Life with Strings Attached

Life
with Strings
Attached

Minnie Lamberth

PARACLETE PRESS
BREWSTER, MASSACHUSETTS

This book is a work of fiction. Names, characters, and incidents are either products of the author's imagination or are used fictitiously. Any resemblance to actual events, or persons, living or dead, is coincidental.

Library of Congress Cataloging-in-Publication Data
Lamberth, Minnie.
  Life with strings attached / by Minnie Lamberth
      p. cm.
  ISBN 1-55725-416-8
  1. Girls—Fiction. 2. Alabama—Fiction. 3. Preaching—Fiction.
  I. Title.

  PS3612.A5467L54 2005
  813'.6—dc22

                    2004026238

2005 First printing

ISBN 1-55725-416-8

10 9 8 7 6 5 4 3 2 1

Published by Paraclete Press
Brewster, Massachusetts
www.paracletepress.com

Printed in the United States of America

In memory of Jane Kershaw Lamberth

one

* * *

When I saw the Second Coming of Christ, or what I thought was the Second Coming, I had been a Christian for two days. I was seven. My brother, Franklin, was ten. It was early dusk on a Tuesday in April 1972, and we were in the backseat of a brown Chevrolet Caprice on the way to a baseball field to see Franklin play in a Little League game. Daddy was driving.

"Tie your shoes, Franklin," Momma said from the front seat.

One thing about Franklin: at any important time in his life, you could count on his shoelaces to be untied. Momma knew this instinctively and reminded him without any need to see his feet.

Another thing about Franklin was his capacity for surprise. "Oh," he said, as if this were the first time he had noticed untied shoelaces and was unfamiliar with the connection between his actions and his feet.

As Franklin bent over to tie his laces, I turned toward the window. A soft glow, a halo, peered above the treetops along the roadway, and my heart quickened. "Jesus is coming again," Brother John had said on Sunday. "He's coming soon, and we'll see Him like lightning across a starry sky."

1

For two days already, I had been waiting. Now, surely this soft glow was the Second Coming of Christ, and I was seeing it first.

"It's . . ." was all I was able to say when, at an opening in the trees, the light grew very bright. The lights did, I should say. They stood in rows of four on tall wooden poles.

"It's what?" asked Franklin.

"It's the ball field."

"I can see that," Franklin said. But that was the only part he saw. He missed the split second before—an accelerating anticipation punctured by disappointment and falling into a place of hopeful acceptance. That split second sums up a lot more than you might imagine.

Oh, well. Then as now, life moves on. In one moment I was convinced I had seen the Second Coming; in the next, I was at the concession stand buying a hot dog, vaguely aware of the presence of knowledge and the absence of clarity.

There is nothing more elusive than religious faith: it can be the most real thing you've ever known, the brightest light you've ever seen. And at any moment, you may wonder if it was only a mirage, a ball field in the distance.

This was my prayer for many years: "Forgive me my doubt as I forgive those who doubt against me." It started because I had misheard, and incorrectly memorized, a line in the Lord's Prayer, "Forgive us our debts as we forgive those who debt against us." By the time I understood the correct version, I had internalized my original plea and

2

couldn't stop saying it. "Forgive me my doubt as I forgive those who doubt against me" ran through my mind like an unceasing prayer.

I have been trying to remember what it was that I knew before I began to doubt. I think you cannot know doubt unless you know belief. Therefore, to find this time before doubt, I'd have to go back to the beginning of belief, probably as far back as the beginning of me. But I'd rather start just after my seventh birthday, on the day I joined the Wellton Baptist Church of Wellton, Alabama.

This was a time when a door opened into my soul. The promises of God were there for the taking, and I took. When I did, I found out about giving back. It also became clear that there are obstacles to both give and take, some of which we can see but others that are hidden, at least to a child's eyes.

On the sunny but cool Easter morning following shortly after my seventh birthday, I skipped up the concrete church steps, wearing blue buckle-up dress shoes, white lace socks, a blue and white sailor dress, and a white cardigan sweater with the cuffs turned back. My feet lifted easily; they tapped in a rhythm, a rhythm countered by that of my parents and my brother and of all the others walking in their individual believers' tempos: hurried, reverent, sleepy, uncomfortable, or self-assured.

3

I was in that last category, wearing the perfect Easter outfit as I was. With my light brown hair bouncing (having been rolled overnight in pink foam curlers), I was ready to burst into song. Music had become important to me. I was learning the piano at home, playing by ear in my own rite of communion. Only the distress it would have created among the masses prevented me from heading straight for the powerful organ to press the notes I'd learned so far. Fortunately even a seven-year-old knows a thing or two about propriety and decorum.

Moving toward the middle of the sanctuary to an empty row, I entered first, followed by Momma, Franklin, and Daddy. I immediately doubled back, crawling over all three to be on the end. I wanted to hang my head to the side of the pew for a better view.

On Easter, or any Sunday for that matter, I liked going to church. Maybe it was that I liked my hair, shoes, and dress, or maybe I thought the sanctuary was one step closer to heaven, I'm not sure, but I loved the ceremony of the worship service and thought the room itself was lovely. The pews were dark brown with white painted wood at each end; the pew cushions and carpet in the aisles and at the pulpit were a deep red; the walls and doors were white. Four gold chandeliers served as accents for a dozen stained glass windows—six on each side.

Soon a white-robed choir entered a loft behind the pulpit like angels heralding the arrival of the preacher.

John Pierce, the one arriving, was a fastidious man. He wore a gray suit with a red silk tie tightly knotted at the collar of a white starched shirt; the sleeves had monogrammed cuffs. His wavy blond hair was both combed and tousled, a calculated effect that seemed to work and that I admired. A lot of folks called him Brother John; Daddy called him Banker John (but not to his face).

I remember two other things now: Daddy called choir robes angel costumes, and he said the collection plates were like Frisbees, only with felt cloth inside. After the deacons counted the money on Sunday afternoons, Daddy told me, they would stand in the empty parking lot and throw the plates to each other. I had a feeling he was teasing me, but for years I kept this picture in my head: men in suits in an empty parking lot throwing collection plates like they were Frisbees.

This was to be a big day, and not just because it was Easter. Behind-the-scenes workings had put the plan in place for Franklin to become a Christian. Myra Hamilton, head of children's Sunday school, had called our house the week before to express her concern that, of a dozen boys and girls in the class she taught, Franklin was the only one who had not yet accepted Jesus. When she had asked if he was ready, his reply startled her.

"No, ma'am," Franklin answered politely. "I don't want to go to heaven." That's what prompted the call.

Momma hung up the phone in the den as Daddy came around the corner dressed, ironically, like one of the disciples.

He was playing Bartholomew in the Last Supper play that night, so he had colored on a black beard, fashioned a robe out of a bed sheet, and tied it at the waist with a woven curtain cord, which he had taken to calling his Bible belt.

When Momma told Daddy of Mrs. Hamilton's concern, they both went to Franklin's room to talk to him. What they found out—with Momma appearing as herself and Daddy appearing as Bartholomew—was that Franklin's deep-seated fear of heaven was based on his notion that it would be nothing more than a long church service. He was afraid he would have to spend eternity in a clip-on tie.

Daddy assured him that in heaven he would not have to wear a tie and sit still unless he wanted to wear a tie and sit still. Franklin smiled at the ludicrous idea that he would *want* to wear a tie and sit still, and he began to relax.

"You know what I would have told Myra Hamilton?" I heard Daddy later say to Momma. "I would have said, 'Franklin doesn't want to go to heaven because he's afraid you'll be the head of all the committees.'"

"That's why I'm glad I answered the phone," Momma said.

The worship service was a well-organized event. The preacher made announcements, the congregation sang a hymn, the choir sang, someone read from the Bible, someone sang a solo, and ushers passed collection plates through the pews.

6

"Put this in for me," Daddy whispered as he handed over a five-dollar bill. That was a sum of money I would have preferred to keep for myself, which prompted my hesitation when a collection plate was in front of me, which prompted Momma to poke me in the shoulder.

At her helpful reminder, I dropped the bill on top of several dollars and envelopes and watched the plate as it passed from hand to hand until an usher retrieved it at the end of our pew and passed it down the next. Then several ushers with plates met as a group at the back of the church and returned together to the altar in the front. I tried to follow the usher holding the plate with our five-dollar bill, but when they stacked the plates on top of each other, I lost track. As the head usher took the stacked plates through a side door, the others took seats next to their wives in the congregation.

This was a system that, as far as I knew, had no variation. Neither did the next part have any variation: Brother John took the pulpit and talked for twenty minutes about Jesus. As he began to close, he reminded us of Jesus' imminent return, then issued an invitation to become a Christian.

"I want to talk to the members of the congregation who are separated from God," Brother John said. "We do not know what will happen tomorrow or next week. We do not know how long we have on this earth. If you have not accepted Jesus as your Savior, if you have not joined the church, I want to issue this invitation to you to come forward during the closing hymn.

"Don't be afraid of how it will look. Don't be afraid to walk down the aisle by yourself, for you are surely not alone. We are all children of God. We come as children to God, and He welcomes us as His children. Now let us pray."

We bowed our heads and closed our eyes as organ music played softly. In a rare moment for a seven-year-old, I was absolutely still.

"Father," Brother John said, "to those who are praying with me today, allow me to say for You, to each one here, you are His child, and He loves you very much, and He wants you to come forward."

As I basked in the warmth of Brother John's baritone intonations, an idea began to form in my mind—an idea of loving-kindness, of omniscient sweetness. I remember a strong sense of feeling chosen, and by a friendly Higher Being at that. Convinced of my own specialness, when Brother John said "amen," I opened my eyes and knew in an instant: I was bound for the Promised Land.

"If you want the blessed assurance of life everlasting," the preacher said, "come forward during the closing hymn, and we will welcome you as children of God."

The sounds of the organ filled the sanctuary as Henry Morton, the music director, held up his arms; the congregation stood to sing. In my state of equal parts confusion and certainty, I watched Franklin. Whatever move he took, I was taking. He shifted his weight to the left, then the right. He turned one foot on its side, then on its heel.

Suddenly the chains of his spirit were unshackled, and he was walking down the aisle on his way toward eternal life. Just as suddenly, as if we were tied together with invisible rope, I was yanked down the aisle with him. Franklin didn't realize I followed him until he got to the front of the church, shook hands with the preacher, and turned to face the congregation.

"What are you doing here?" he asked under his breath.

"I'm accepting Jesus," I said. A moment's reaction in Franklin's face let me know that he had not counted on a little sister pestering him for all of his mortal life and, following that, all through eternity. But he shook it off and turned his attention to the congregation whose attention was on us.

"Ladies and gentlemen," Brother John said, "I would like for you to welcome Franklin and Hannah Hayes, who have come today to make professions of faith. They are the children of Martin and Mary, and we are so pleased they have responded to this invitation to walk with Jesus."

Dozens of members of the congregation came up afterward to greet us as a new brother and sister in Christ. "You are such precious children," one lady said as she hugged me, "and I know the Lord is smiling."

That afternoon and the next day at school I told almost everyone what had happened, that I was a child of God and had become a member of His church and was going to be baptized in the faith. A lot of people weren't nearly as interested as you would think they'd be. "That's nice," they said. How could they not see it? I was practically announcing that I was a close relative of the most famous person on earth and, furthermore, I was now living my life in the full belief that I was the Lord's favorite.

The neighborhood we lived in didn't have definite building patterns. Some of the houses were two-story wooden, some one-story brick. A few had gravel driveways, the others had concrete. Even with the differences in style, the homes were woven together like a community, and there were lots of trees—a mix of magnolia, maple, dogwood, and pine.

We were on Evergreen Drive, a dead end off Southview. Nothing new had come to Southview since 1955; it was a winding and settled residential road. But Evergreen had an unfinished quality. Our home was the third of seven houses on our side; five others were across the street, with a vacant lot at the end.

My brother had some playmates on the street—the Fords, a family with three boys lived at the corner on the other side, and there was a high school majorette directly across from us who sometimes gave them the time of day when not practicing baton twirls in her front yard. For me, there was Debbie Sellers, two years older, who lived on our side at the corner, and Sammy Morris, a red-haired boy a year younger, who lived on the other side next to the vacant lot. I was not unlike Goldilocks in my view of these options:

"That friend is too old, that friend is too young." But there was another who was just right.

Debbie was strictly an inside girl, preferring to read thick books without pictures, and Sammy had a nervous mother who wouldn't let him stray too far from home lest he pick up bad habits or fall in the dirt. That mostly left me following my brother and his friends around until I got on their nerves, then retreating to the affections of my one true friend, my beagle Pumpkin.

Pumpkin had floppy ears and huge brown eyes, but her finer qualities were found in her sweet disposition, longing heart, and earnest look. With no real sense of the passage of time, she would be happy to see you in one minute; you could turn around and walk through the room a moment later, and she'd be happy to see you all over again.

Pumpkin and I enjoyed some of the same hobbies. On Thursdays, for instance, she was the only one who would watch and wait with me for the garbage men to come to our street. When we heard the brakes of a big green truck squeak at the turn onto Evergreen, Pumpkin was on alert. Her bark was sharp, strong and, as a hound's might be, slightly mournful. With her call to arms, I ran to the yard's edge for a good view. One man drove, two others hung onto the back, hopping off to canvass the neighborhood for cylindrical cans, rolling them down driveways and across pavement, emptying them into the truck's belly, and rolling them back to their places.

Through all of this, there was a lot of hopping on and off the truck and riding to the next stop, which seemed like good work if you could get it. That's probably why being a garbage collector was my first career goal. My parents ignored my pronouncements, "I'm going to ride on a garbage truck when I grow up," knowing full well that I would grow out of this desire. It would become obvious over time that girls did or did not do certain things. That girls did not ride on garbage trucks, for instance, was something I would never need to be told. Momma and Daddy seemed confident that if they fulfilled their parental responsibilities by helping me to watch my grammar and mind my manners, there would be no need to tell me I didn't want to ride on a garbage truck when I grew up. On that matter, they were right. But until I reached the appropriate level of maturity, I practiced for my future career whenever I went to the Piggly Wiggly with Momma.

"Let me put the groceries in the buggy," I pleaded with Momma on Saturday afternoon as she pulled a cart from its row. Stepping onto the front, I grabbed hold of the buggy's bars. Each time she picked up a can of green beans or a tomato or detergent, I hopped off the front, dropped the item she selected into the basket, and hopped back on for the ride to the next stop.

Franklin was with us too; he entertained himself in another way—by picking up things off the shelves and asking, "Can we have this? Will you get us one of these?"

"No, put that back. We're not getting that today," Momma said over and over as we made our slow pilgrimage through the store. I was busy working on my imaginary garbage truck, paying no attention to Franklin, and was therefore stunned when I found out that someone else had been paying him very careful attention. A man I didn't see followed behind us with his cart, and each time Franklin picked up something and asked if we could have it, the man put the same item into his basket. After he'd checked out, he handed this sack of goodies to Franklin while Momma was waiting for the bagging of her own groceries. The rustling of the paper sack and the exclamations of surprise from my brother snapped me back into the real world. I stepped off my garbage truck and stared with incredulity at a jar of pickles which Franklin held as if it was his very own.

"Where did you get that?" I demanded.

"A man gave it to me," Franklin said. "He gave me this other stuff, too." When I peered into the bag and saw potato chips, cookies, and a soft drink, I was impressed.

"Wow. What man gave that to you?"

"I don't know. That man." Franklin pointed toward the store's entrance, and I turned to see for myself, but caught only a glimpse as automatic doors closed behind the man's back.

"No fair," I said. "Momma, that's not fair."

"No, it's not fair, Hannah," she said, "but I'm sure Franklin will be glad to share with you. Won't you, Franklin?"

14

"Yes, ma'am," he said. In the car, we opened the bag of chips, but Momma said the pickles would have to wait. When she pulled into our driveway, Franklin's hand was on the car door. "I've got to tell Daddy."

"Slow down, Franklin," Momma said.

"Daddy!" Franklin yelled into the kitchen. "There was a man in the grocery store who bought all the things I wanted!" Daddy reached to get a grocery bag from Momma's arms as she walked into the kitchen.

"What happened?" he asked.

"Franklin kept asking for different things as we were going through the store, and I kept telling him no. Apparently, there was a man with a cart behind us who picked up the things Franklin asked for and when we were leaving, he presented Franklin with a sack full of snacks."

"My goodness, Franklin," Daddy said. "It seems like a Snack Angel is looking out for you."

"I didn't know the man," Momma continued. "I was kind of embarrassed, but Franklin was so happy, I couldn't tell him we couldn't keep it."

"The Bible says remember to entertain strangers because we may be entertaining angels without knowing it," Daddy said.

"Hannah was riding a garbage truck and Franklin was asking, 'Can we have this? Can we have that?' I have no doubt the Snack Angel found us very entertaining."

These were the old days, before you'd have that reservation in the back of your mind that any man who helped a boy could be a pervert with bad intentions. As far as I know, this was simply a man remembering what it was like to be a boy. I didn't see the Snack Angel, but it was a powerful notion to me that someone might see your sincere longings and provide a way to help you achieve them. Naturally, the receiving end is where I thought I might best fit. It didn't occur to me to wonder about that providing end.

Our house was made of bricks coated with white paint. In its twenty years the house had been painted several times, and thick coats made wooden windows hard to raise. But I yanked them open anyway; I liked to hear the sounds of the neighborhood—cars on gravel driveways, children peddling plastic three-wheelers, the soft murmur of neighbors talking with each other or about each other. What I miss most is the sound of rain. Our carport had an aluminum roof on which several steady pings of water would announce the coming of rain.

"It's starting to rain," Momma yelled as she brought in the last of the groceries. I stood in a chair at the kitchen table, where the groceries had been placed, and unloaded whatever items I could lift from the sacks. I wasn't tall enough yet to put anything on the shelves; that was Franklin's job.

"Sorry I have to get back to my work, Mary," Daddy said.

"That's okay. I know you're busy."

Daddy walked down the hallway, as I hopped off the chair and followed. In the corner of the master bedroom there was a desk. That's where I found him penciling notes on a yellow legal pad.

"What are you doing, Daddy?" I asked.

"I have a presentation next week," he said without looking up. "I'm getting my thoughts together."

I remembered that I too had a presentation the next week and felt it would be wise to prepare myself. I retreated to my parents' bathroom, which had lately become my own private studio, to practice my performance for the Goldilocks Revue. In an end-of-the-year class musical, I had a role as the baby bear. I had three lines of my own, and there were several songs to sing. My practice stage was a footstool I used when washing hands and brushing teeth; my audience was the mirror above the sink.

"Somebody's been eating my porridge," I said to no one in particular. "And it's all gone." Distant thunder accompanied my baby bear practice; the smell of steam rising from pavement came through an open window. Suddenly the strength of the rain increased. Imagining it to be the sound of prolonged applause, I paused for intermission.

Nothing has ever been so fascinating to me as my own image in the mirror. As I looked straight into my eyes, my

17

eyes looked straight back at me. I couldn't get a full view of myself, only the front of my face. When I turned my face to the left, I could see part of one side. When I turned my face to the right, I could see part of another side. I could not see my whole self from any angle. I studied this reflection until my attention was diverted by motion.

"Daddy?" I called. He poked his head into the bathroom.

"What is it, Hannah?"

"Which is really me? The one in the mirror or the one looking at the one in the mirror?"

Daddy came up beside me and placed his reflection next to mine. We were a contrast in color. His dark brown hair, tanned skin, green eyes, sharp angles were not at all like the fair skin and roundness of my own reflection. My features were like my mother's—blue eyes, full cheeks, three freckles on the nose, all surrounded by light brown hair.

"That's the funny thing about mirrors," Daddy said. "We think of mirrors as things that tell us how we look. They are in fact exactly how we do not look. They are actually the opposite of us."

"You mean I don't look like the girl in the mirror?"

"You look similar to the girl in the mirror; others might mistake you for the girl in the mirror. But if you study the whole thing carefully, you'll see that your hair in real life is not parted on what you see as the left side, but is parted on what everybody else sees as the right side.

18

That's the strange thing about life. We see ourselves the opposite of how others see us."

I looked at Daddy's part in his hair in the mirror, then I turned back to look at his part in real life. It was the opposite.

"Then which one is me?" I asked again.

"You're the one that's always you on the inside," he said. "That sweet little face on the outside will change. But what happens on the inside, as you grow in your mind and in your heart, will help you be who you truly are, and eventually that's what everyone else will see."

"Then what are mirrors for?" I asked.

"To make sure we don't have spinach between our teeth."

"But I don't like spinach," I protested.

"Then I recommend that you not keep it between your teeth."

three

here were always people who were missing, whose absence left a hole or set certain things into motion, and you wonder in what way the world may have changed, or stayed the same, had that vacancy never occurred. In our house, the evidence of people unseen was kept in the living room, which meant a different set of operating rules. I could enter if I was looking for Pumpkin or walking through to the front door, but I was not to dawdle or bump into anything. A denied object becomes an irresistible force, to be sure.

The sound of paw nails tapping in the hallway moved toward the living room, and I followed. With the rain retreating, streams of sunshine poured through wooden blinds creating a mixture of brightness and shadow. An oversized shadow of the blinds fell across a bookcase, and in the opposite corner everything was dark except for the glow of a soft lamp on our piano.

A brown wooden upright, the piano had been handed down from my grandmother on my mother's side. Both of my mother's parents had died before I was born, and there were a number of things around the house, particularly in the living room, which were explained in this way: "I got that from Momma." "That came from Daddy." Those phrases had no emotional context for me. As far as I knew, the world started when I was born, and the piano may as well have always been in our living room.

I was convinced that it held hidden knowledge. Because of that, and in clear violation of family policy, I had begun to dawdle. Weeks earlier, I had first pulled myself onto the bench and run my fingers longingly across the ivory keys. I did not press down. "Momma," I had called, "how do you get the music out of the piano?"

My mother's voice returned from the kitchen. "It's not in the piano. It's in the bench. Lift the top of the bench. The music's inside."

Slipping off the piano bench, I lifted the seat to find books and sheets of paper. This was the way it often was with me. I had asked a specific question, "how do you get the music out of the piano," meaning "how do you get the sound of music, the melody of music, out of the piano," and my mother directed me to books and sheets of paper.

Grabbing a thick hymnal out of the seat of the bench, I flipped through the pages to see things I could not read. The bench's lid fell shut with a muted thud. I laid the hymnal on top of the bench, pulled myself on top of the hymnal, and poised my fingers on the smooth surface of the keys. Still I did not press down.

Momma poked her head in the room. "Playing the piano is difficult," she said.

"Yes, it is," I agreed.

"The sun's out now. Why don't you run outside, get some fresh air, go do something?"

"Can you play this piano?" I asked.

"I took a few lessons as a child." Placing her finger on a key, she said, "This is middle C. If you press this key and hold it until you count to four, you're playing a whole note."

With my right forefinger, I pressed middle C. It made a fine sound, I thought. Momma pressed a few more keys. They made a melody. I watched, fascinated. "Can you teach me?" I asked.

"Place your fingers like this," she said, spreading them over the keys. I did. She pressed each in turn, making the same melody. I loved the sound. But when I tried it without her help, it came out wrong.

"Teach me again," I pleaded.

"You can learn one day," she said. "Perhaps next year you can take lessons."

"And then I'll be able to play it?"

"You can do anything you set your mind to."

The wisdom of the ages was encapsulated in that last statement. When you know something in your mind and in your heart, it is no less than the knowledge of the workings of the universe. It is everything you are and will be. And it was in these early formations of understanding the things you can set your mind to that I began to recognize something important. I was called by God to do His work. Playing the piano seemed like a stepping stone for getting to that special place. Its link with worship as unmistakable, since it had been a part of every church service I had attended. Yet on this particular day I gave a name to my call that was quite different.

I'd followed Pumpkin into the living room, stopping at the piano long enough to press middle C. The simple sound wasn't a melody, but I do know it was a prayer. The secrets of a life dedicated to God could very well be within this instrument, and I wanted to know what those secrets were.

"Don't dawdle in the living room, Hannah," my mother said as she looked in from the kitchen. My single-note prayer had prompted her attention. "The sun's out now. Why don't you run and play?"

I carefully closed the cover over the keys—my way of saying "amen"—and called to Pumpkin. She eased her way from under the living room sofa and followed me outside. From the porch there were seven concrete steps to take to get to the yard. As we reached the bottom, I broke into a run.

"Here, girl," I called to Pumpkin. I knew her weakness for giving chase, and sure enough she was at my heels as I circled around the front yard. When we went around again, however, she adjusted her strategy, aiming straight through the legs. It foiled us both. I tripped and fell on the grass; Pumpkin yelped. I didn't actually kick her, but it must have

23

felt like I kicked her when my shoe accidentally touched her with some degree of force.

She was a forgiving dog.

Plopping down on the grass, I hugged her close. "Pumpkin, do you know Jesus?" I asked. "He's our friend."

She looked at me without speaking, so I continued.

"I'm His witness on earth, until He comes back."

No comment yet from Pumpkin.

"Do you know what that means?" I persisted. "It means I'm a preacher. Well, I'm not one now actually, but when I grow up. When I'm big."

Looking straight at me with her big brown eyes, Pumpkin spoke no word, but she did nod.

Our conversation was interrupted when Franklin walked into the yard. He was holding an empty pickle jar—clear evidence that he had shared his pickles with his friends, but not with me.

"I didn't get any pickles," I complained.

"Here. You can have the rest," Franklin said, holding out the jar. But it contained only juice, and he knew that. Still, I took it. There's no need to refuse a jar just for spite. Uncapping it, I poured the green liquid onto the ground. When Franklin walked inside, I bounded up the front steps and called for Momma.

"Will you make this into a bug jar for me?" I yelled into the living room. Momma was soon in the doorway.

"Okay, but wait right here," she said.

24

As Momma took the jar into the kitchen, dogs barking in the distance called to Pumpkin. She barked in return, and I grabbed her collar to keep her close.

"Stay with me, Pumpkin. We're going to play." Barking again, she broke from my grip and rushed toward the backyard to find the other dogs. "Pumpkin, wait!" I urged. But she wasn't listening. I watched her turn the corner of the house as Momma returned with a jar that had been rinsed. Three holes were poked in the jar's top.

"Here you go," she said. "Now run along and collect some bugs. Play outside for awhile."

"Will you come look for bugs with me?"

"Maybe later. Why don't you see how many bugs you can find on your own, or go play with Sammy. Or Debbie. You really need to be outside enjoying this fresh air."

"Do you need to be outside?"

"I need to be in the kitchen, or else we will have nothing for supper and a little girl and all of her family will have to go to bed hungry. Now run along, sweetie, okay?"

And so I ran along, or rather walked along, looking for bugs under large stones near the driveway. I found none worth collecting. Moving to the edge of our front yard, I followed the sidewalk to the end of the street. Sammy was on the other side playing in the vacant lot next to his house. Momma said Sammy, with little red curls all over his head, had the prettiest hair of anyone on the street, but I didn't see what was so special about it.

25

"What are you doing?" I called.

"Digging to China. Want to help me?" It was common knowledge around that time that if you started digging in America and kept digging all the way through the earth, you would end up in China.

"Okay," I shrugged, crossing over to the lot.

"I only have one shovel," he said, holding up a gardener's spade.

"I can use my jar."

We scooped up small mounds of dirt with a jar and spade, but made little progress. "It takes a long time to get to China," Sammy said.

"How long have you been digging?"

"Since yesterday."

In Sammy's world, yesterday didn't actually mean yesterday. Any day that was a previous day was yesterday and any day that was a future day was tomorrow. I, on the other hand, was a whole year older. Having learned the basics of keeping track of time—the days of the week in particular—I liked to show off.

"Today's Saturday," I said. Sammy looked at me like he didn't care what day it was, so I kept digging with my bug jar. In the distance, a car turned onto our street, and almost simultaneously, Sammy's mother stepped out of their front door.

"Here comes Mr. Stevens," she called to us, "so watch out."

Mr. Stevens was a man who was down on his luck. He lived alone in a house across the street. His wife used to live with him, but she had gone to visit relatives several years ago and hadn't gotten back yet. And his children didn't turn out well. They were some acorns that hadn't fallen far from the tree. Still, he was a friendly man. When he pulled into his driveway and got out of his car, he waved to the three of us, and we waved back.

"Sammy, you better come inside now," his mother said. "Look at how dirty you've gotten. We better get you cleaned up before your daddy gets home. Tell Hannah you can play with her tomorrow."

"Tomorrow's Sunday," I said.

"You can't play on Sunday?" she asked.

When I had said "Tomorrow's Sunday," I hadn't meant it in a way that meant I couldn't play on Sunday. I was simply showing off again about knowing my days of the week. This is what pride will do to you, I suppose.

"I can play on Sundays after church," I said.

"Well, maybe Sammy will see you tomorrow then. After church."

Sammy and his mother went inside their house, and I was left in the lot by myself. I scooped a few more mounds of dirt, but grew quickly uninterested in digging to China alone. When a buzzing sound drifted through the neighborhood, I was glad to hear it. The streetlights were coming on, and that was my signal for going home.

27

I stood, brushing off the dirt in my lap. As I crossed back to the sidewalk on our side, a long, strong whistle pierced the neighborhood. Mr. Ford was calling his boys in for supper. He never had to call them by name. He simply stood at his backdoor and whistled, and they knew to come home.

I was three houses away from our house when I spotted Franklin at the end of our street. Earl Ford, Franklin's closest neighborhood friend, was walking into his front door as Franklin turned toward home. When Franklin saw me, he began to run, and I began to run, passing one house, then another. As Franklin sailed into our yard a few paces ahead, my legs were like jelly, and I couldn't catch my breath. "I won," he yelled over his shoulder as he headed to the backdoor.

By the time I reached our driveway and slowed to a walk, my side was hurting, my face was red, and I was panting like a puppy dog. And then I remembered: I had left my bug jar in the hole I was digging to China. I wanted to go back to get it, but there was a boundary issue that I needed to resolve. Technically, I had already gotten home. If I had remembered before I had gotten home, I could have just turned back. But if I were home already, I couldn't leave again without permission. Not wanting to waste any precious daylight before rescuing my jar, I picked up the pace again and ran to the backdoor.

"Momma," I yelled breathlessly when I stepped into the kitchen, "I left my bug jar in the hole in the vacant lot, and I have to go back to get it."

Momma pulled the door closed behind me. "Hannah, how about we use our inside voices when we're inside."

"But I need to go back and get my bug jar!"

"Not tonight. It's suppertime. Go wash up."

"Okay," I said, disappointed. When I passed Franklin in the hallway, he bumped his shoulder into mine. He did it on purpose, but he said "excuse me" as if it were an accident.

"You did that on purpose," I said.

He shrugged. "It was an accident."

"No, it wasn't, and it wasn't an accident that you ate all the pickles either. You did it on purpose."

"Settle down, you two," Momma called from the kitchen.

When I got back into the kitchen after washing my hands, Momma pointed to the table. "Put a napkin at each place, won't you?" I pulled open the napkin drawer as Daddy began putting plates around the table.

"What were you and Sammy doing this afternoon?" he asked.

"Digging to China."

"China!" Franklin howled, taking his seat at the table. "You can't dig to China."

"Can to," I snorted. "Can't you, Daddy?"

"I can't say it's impossible, but nobody has figured out a way to do it yet," Daddy said. "Who knows? When I was a boy, landing on the moon was thought to be impossible,

29

but a lot of people worked hard and made it happen. So why do you want to dig to China anyway?"

"I don't know," I admitted.

"Well," Daddy said, "I think if you want to do something that difficult, you should know why you want to do it."

four

In 1972 Wellton reached a population of ten thousand, thanks in part to a Chamber of Commerce contest. The population count had come in just under five digits in the last census, so a city statistician did some figuring and, based on average births and deaths, was able to pinpoint a month when Wellton might reach ten thousand. At a meeting of the directors the summer before, the statistician announced that the milestone would occur around the middle of March.

Daddy sensed an opportunity for promoting community spirit and proposed an idea for a baby watch at Wellton Hospital on March 15, to recognize what would presumably be the town's ten-thousandth citizen. The first baby born on that day would be the winner. The idea was praised at first, until one of the directors expressed a fear that it might encourage marginal couples to have a baby they couldn't take care of just to get their photographs in *The Wellton Courier*. The Chamber decided to have a contest, but to keep it quiet until it was actually won. Which didn't work. The directors told their wives and friends, and soon it was the most well-known secret in town.

The Manns, who lived two houses down from us, were the winners. It was between them and the McMillans, a couple from our church. Both mothers-to-be went into labor early that morning, but the Manns edged out the McMillans by thirty minutes. The next week the paper ran a photograph of the happy couple and their new baby boy on the front page, spoofing the lack of secrecy with this headline: "Every man, woman, and child knows the Manns have a child."

As Daddy liked to say, "Only in Wellton." I don't know if that phrase was intended to promote community spirit, but I know that I wrapped myself around the thought, as if the "only-ness" of my city was a good and special thing.

Wellton had its beginnings at the corner of Piedmont and Earlie. Earlie was from a Mr. Earlie who sometime in the mid-1800s established a general store at a crossroads not far from Montgomery.

The Wellton Bank and Earlie's Department Store, each descendants of early Earlie enterprises, began at this corner of Piedmont and Earlie and extended for the full length of downtown, which was about one city block. Piedmont, on the other hand, was not from a Mr. Piedmont, but from the soil that had gotten here even before Mr. Earlie.

Wellton and its surroundings had once been a place for mining gold and copper, but that didn't take. What took were the railroad tracks, built through the middle of town parallel to Piedmont and perpendicular to Earlie. Soon more commerce came along, including a half-dozen cotton and knitting mills, one of which was Hamilton Sock Company.

How all of that relates to me is that my father was the sock company's marketing and public relations manager. A part of his publicity was to give socks to schools and organizations, which is the reason Franklin and I had more socks than we could wear.

"I give these things to schools and organizations so that they will like us," Daddy explained to me.

"I like you, Daddy," I said.

"That's good to know. I'll tell Mr. Hamilton that the program is working."

Thomas Charles Hamilton III, a tall, lean man with a grim face, was the company's president. According to Daddy, Mr. Hamilton ate a lot of lemons and that's why he was always in a sour mood. But I suspect that his ill humor came from deep religious convictions. In his fervor to live a godly life, it upset him when people didn't see things the same way he did. His wife, Myra, was like that too. Stella, their seventeen-year-old daughter, was not. She was, bless her heart, a tramp. She wore tight clothes, smoked cigarettes, drank beer, and hung out with wild boys.

"Sometimes the acorn doesn't fall far from the tree," Daddy explained. "But this time, it fell, packed its bags, and ran."

Whenever I thought of Stella, I thought of a tiny acorn with tiny arms and legs and tiny running shoes skedaddling with a tiny overstuffed suitcase.

Wellton, of course, was a religious community, at least that's my perception. If there were nonbelievers in the town, I probably wouldn't have known them if for no other reason than they didn't go to church with me. As far as religious diversity goes, that was mostly defined by some of us being Methodist and some of us being Baptist, although there were a few other denominations in the mix.

The main churches, Wellton Baptist and Wellton Methodist, were side by side in the next block on Earlie. Just across the street, there was a brick building named Myers and Myers, Attorneys-at-Law. The Myers family went way back in Wellton; the father and grandfather of these attorneys-at-law was Milton Myers, who'd had a hand in the city's founding. In fact, he had donated the land for the churches, one of which, a hundred years later, I attended every Sunday.

Wellton Baptist had been led for as long as I'd been born by John Pierce, a lifelong Baptist whose father and father-in-law were Baptist preachers as well. His wife, Shelia, was the organist. Each Sunday she sat on a bench low in the choir loft, watching the proceedings through a rearview mirror affixed to the organ, while Brother John stood in the center of activity, welcoming all in the

34

name of the Lord. Even then I could see that being a preacher was important work.

The Pierces had three children—two daughters, Claire and Brenda, and a son, Ron. Ron, the one in the middle, was the most handsome boy in high school, broad-shouldered and blond. Like many children of preachers, however, he had a wild streak. He was known to drink beer and play guitar, and sometimes on Sunday mornings was late for church. He was friendly though.

"Morning, Mr. and Mrs. Hayes. Hi, Franklin," Ron would say as he passed us by. Then he would pause for a moment and look straight into my eyes. "Hello, Hannah," he'd say, and my heart would pound almost out of my chest.

If we parked in the front lot when we went to church, we entered through the front door. But if we parked in the back lot, we would enter through a side door, walk past the Sunday school area for teenagers, and I could see the man of my dreams.

"Park in the back!" I yelled to Daddy on Sunday morning as the church came into view.

"When did Jesus leave the building and put you in charge?" Daddy asked. But he did as I requested. He turned down an alley beside the church building and pulled into a parking place in the back lot.

As Momma, Daddy, Franklin, and I walked toward the building, we were greeted by the dozen or so high school students who always hung around the covered back entrance.

35

This was usually where old people and mothers with young babies were dropped off, or wives and children when it was raining. I searched for Ron in this crowd, and there he was, right in the middle of the group.

My exultation turned to dismay: he was holding the hand of Stella Hamilton. I was devastated. At this time in our lives—he was seventeen and I was seven—the age difference was too great. But I was growing up so fast, as everyone was telling me. I had been certain Ron would sense my special qualities and wait for me to catch up. Yet here he was holding the hand of, bless her heart, a tramp. I was so shook up I stopped in my tracks. This stopped Momma too because I was holding her hand at the time.

"Come on, Hannah," Momma said as she pulled me forward. "Miss Bertie is waiting for you."

Now, do I really know enough about Miss Bertie to tell you who she was? Probably not, but let's assume I do. She lived on Southview, which made her a neighbor, someone I might see between here and there. She was my Sunday school teacher. And she was old—so old Moses could have been her uncle; Lot's wife might have been in her bridge club.

Miss Bertie wore her white hair in a bun, and whenever she read to us, her head bobbed up and down—up to read from the bottom of her bifocal eyeglasses, down to see her class members from the top of her lenses. Anything that happened between bobs, she could not see.

36

When we'd all arrived for Sunday school, she gathered the class into a circle of wooden chairs. Hers was adult-sized. The half-dozen first graders were in smaller versions of the same chair. "Okay, children," she said, "let's all be quiet and listen to a story from the Bible."

Miss Bertie began a tale of twin brothers, Esau and Jacob, while Jerry and Johnny, two boys sitting next to each other, made faces at Cynthia, who sat across from them. Cynthia stuck her tongue out at Jerry and Johnny. Miss Bertie didn't see any of this; it was between bobs.

"Esau, the older brother, was his father's favorite," Miss Bertie said. "He was a skillful hunter, and Isaac, his father, was very proud of him. Jacob was his mother Rebekah's favorite."

The idea that each of these parents picked one of the kids to like best was troublesome to me. I listened closely to the story.

"It was the custom in those days that the older son receive his father's blessing," Miss Bertie said. "Rebekah had heard Isaac send Esau to hunt and prepare game for him to eat." Stopping for a moment, she asked, "Do any of you know what game is?"

"Checkers is a game," Cynthia said.

"Yes, but I'm talking about a different kind of game," Miss Bertie said. "When I say 'game,' I don't mean something you play. In this case, 'game' is something that hunters kill for food."

"Like a deer?" Johnny asked.

"Like a deer," Miss Bertie replied.

"My daddy hunts deers," Johnny continued. "But he never shot Bambi. He said Bambi lives in another forest."

"Thank you, Johnny. Now, girls and boys, let's move on with the story. Isaac told Esau that when he returned with the game, or the food, Isaac would give him his blessing. Do any of you know what a blessing is?"

This one I knew. "I can say a blessing. I say the blessing at home sometimes before we eat."

"Yes, that can be a kind of blessing," Miss Bertie said, "when you're asking for God's blessing on your food. But I don't mean that kind of blessing. What happens sometimes when you sneeze?"

"They might tell you to wipe your nose?" Jerry asked hesitantly.

"When you sneeze," Miss Bertie continued, "someone might say 'God bless you.' That person is passing on a blessing. Now, Jerry, what if you sneezed, but I told Johnny, 'God bless you?' What if I had in mind that I was going to say 'God bless you' to Johnny, even though you were the one who sneezed?"

Jerry shrugged his shoulders in response.

"Well, that's kind of what Rebekah was thinking. In Bible times, the father would give a special blessing to his oldest son. The blessing was supposed to go to Esau, but Rebekah wanted Jacob to have it. So to keep Esau from

38

getting the blessing, Rebekah cooked some goats for Isaac to eat, and she convinced Jacob to dress up as Esau. Knowing that Isaac was nearly blind, she also placed goat hair on Jacob's neck and hands to make him seem hairy like his brother. Then she sent Jacob in with the meal to receive his father's blessing.

"Now, when Esau got back with the game he had killed, he was upset to hear that Jacob had gotten his blessing, and Esau threatened to kill Jacob. Have any of you ever been very, very mad at your brothers or sisters?"

"Franklin gets mad at me sometimes, but he's not allowed to punch me," I said. "Momma won't let him."

"That's exactly right," Miss Bertie continued. "Rebekah didn't want Esau to hurt Jacob. She told him to go away until it was safe again, and Jacob started running. Now a lot had happened to Jacob that day. He had received his father's blessing. He had made his brother mad. And he was leaving his family and the land that he knew. As he was running away, he became so tired that he wanted to rest. He stopped for the night and tried to make a place to sleep. He didn't have a pillow, so he had to lay his head on a stone. You'd have to be very tired, wouldn't you think, to use a stone for a pillow, and Jacob was very tired.

"Soon he fell asleep. He fell into a very deep sleep and began to have a dream. Jacob dreamed of a ladder leading from earth to heaven. There were angels going up and down the ladder. The Lord was at the top, and the Lord spoke to Jacob, telling him, 'I am your God, and I will do many things for you. Everyone will be blessed through you and your children and your children's children. I'm going to watch over you wherever you go and I'm going to bring you back to this land.'

"When Jacob woke up from his dream, he knew that he must be in a holy place because the Lord had spoken to him. He took the stone he had been sleeping on, poured oil over it, and made a vow, which is like a promise. He said that if God would look after him while he was on this long journey, then he would come back to his father's house, and when he did that, the land he was on would become the Lord's house.

"With God's help, he was coming back, and he left that stone as a symbol of his promise to return."

After church, we had lunch at home, then I slipped into play clothes for an afternoon of leisure. When I reached the den, Daddy was on the couch reading the newspaper, so I plopped down next to him. I'd been thinking about the story Miss Bertie had told us. Parts of it weren't clear to me. What I knew was that I'd heard a story about a family—a momma, a daddy, and two children. Within this unit, things had somehow gotten out of order, and Jacob was running.

"Daddy, is it okay to trick God into talking to you?" I asked.

"I don't think it's possible to trick God, Hannah."

"Will God bless you even if you aren't the oldest son?"

"Of course."

"Oh." I thought about that for a minute. Then another problem occurred to me.

"Daddy," I asked, "can girls be preachers?"

"I suppose so," Daddy said as he lowered his paper and turned toward me. "I haven't seen it, but that doesn't mean it doesn't happen. Wellton is not the whole world anyway. Something could be happening in another part of the country—or another part of the world—that's not happening here. So just because it hasn't happened here, doesn't mean it can't happen."

"What if I get called?" I asked. "Will I have to go away, like Jacob?" That seemed so scary to me; I loved my parents, my neighborhood, even my brother. I couldn't bear the thought of leaving.

"If you get called," Daddy said, "you need to find out, first, who's calling."

"What does that mean?"

"There's a difference in being called by God and being called by a person. Someone who gets a call has to be prepared to stir up trouble. So you have to know for sure who's calling you to stir up trouble."

"Why does somebody have to stir up trouble?" I asked. In my whole life, I had never been allowed to stir up trouble—no talking in class, no running in the hallways, no

41

speaking out of turn. I didn't see how a call from God could free me from the many admonitions to not stir up trouble.

"Well . . . ," Daddy said. He stretched the word in the way people do who don't know which words are coming next. "God communicates to the individual. As far as I can tell, He rarely issues an All Points Bulletin. It would be a lot easier if He said to large crowds, 'I want Hannah to be a preacher.' Instead, He speaks to the individual and the individual has to speak to the crowd. The individual has to say, 'God told me He wants me to be a preacher.' The problem comes when someone yells back, 'But that's not what God told me! God told me He *doesn't* want you to be a preacher.'

"It's a conundrum," Daddy said. "It's definitely a conundrum."

"Do you think someone will start yelling if I get called?" I asked.

"Where there's religion, there's always yelling."

f i v e
⊛

When I walked toward Sammy's house to get my bug jar, Ricky Mann was standing with his parents at their car. The new baby boy had gotten christened that morning at the Methodist church, so Ricky and Sylvia had had a big lunch with both sets of parents. In religious life there aren't many things that can't be celebrated or mourned with a big lunch.

"Can I hold the baby, Mr. Ricky?" I yelled, running toward him.

"He's sleeping right now, Hannah. Why don't you wait a little while until he's up. Y'all can have a good talk."

"Babies don't talk, Mr. Ricky."

"Oh, *he* does, Hannah." Ricky winked at his parents. "He's as smart as a whip, this boy. Ever since he floated down from heaven, he's been telling us how to run the house, and, believe me, we've been doing what he says."

Ricky's mother reached to hug him. "See you later, son," she said, patting him on his back. Turning to get in the car, she added, "and nice to see you, Hannah."

"Yes, ma'am," I said.

"Y'all be good, now. Love y'all." Ricky waved good-bye to his parents, lingering in the yard as his father backed out

43

of the driveway. When the car turned the corner at the end of the street, he pulled a cigarette and lighter out of his shirt pocket. Cupping his hands over the flame, Ricky shook his head.

"I don't care how old you get, Hannah," he said. "You can't ever smoke in front of your parents."

"You can't?" I asked. This was a grown man I was talking to, and I was surprised to hear him say something like that.

"Sure can't. Especially your momma." He drew a puff on his cigarette as he looked down to me. "Where you headed this afternoon?"

"I'm going to the vacant lot to get my bug jar out of the hole we were digging to China."

He nodded. "Well, alright then. Come back later and you can hold little 10K." The baby's real name was Christopher, but Ricky had been calling him 10K as a nickname, in honor of his having been our ten-thousandth citizen.

"Yes, sir," I said, heading back to the sidewalk.

"But don't bring any bugs with you."

"I won't," I promised.

My bug jar was right where I'd left it, and still in good shape despite an overnight stay outdoors. Emptying out the dirt, I grabbed the top and screwed it back on. Sammy's house looked dark and there was no car, so I didn't stop. When I crossed the street, Pumpkin was coming toward me on the sidewalk.

"Pumpkin! What are you doing down here?" She wagged her tail, but offered no explanation for having left home without permission. I reached for her ears and looked her in the eyes. "You don't need to be so far from home. Let's go back," I said with a quick pat. "We'll play in the yard."

"Come on, Pumpkin," I said as I held my bug jar tight and started a run toward home. "Come, girl." Yipping at my heels, Pumpkin followed me all the way to our front yard. "Come on," I called, and we went around the house to the patio in the back.

I placed my bug jar on the window sill, next to one of Pumpkin's sock toys. Daddy had made the toy by putting one old sock inside another and tying the open end. "Here, you go, girl," I said, offering it to Pumpkin. "Here you go." She grabbed one end with her teeth, pulled and growled, while I pulled and growled too.

"Hey, puppy dog Hannah," Franklin said when he turned the corner.

"I'm *not* a puppy dog," I exclaimed. "I am playing with Pumpkin."

Franklin shrugged. Looking around the patio, he asked, "Have you seen my basketball?" I ignored his question, buying myself some time.

"Well, have you seen my basketball or not?" An answer was being forced out, and I had to choose.

"No," I said.

There was a reason for my lie. Franklin had laughed at me the last time he found me with his basketball, and I did not want to face that again. I had been in my room, pretending that I was going to have a baby just like Sylvia Mann, and the basketball had been under my shirt.

"Hey, look at Fatso," he had said when he walked by.

I did not like being called Fatso, but I had no ready defense. In the way you know things without being told, it seemed preferable to have Franklin mistake me for a girl pretending to be fat rather than a girl pretending to be pregnant.

Since then, I had played this game once more. But the basketball fell out of my shirt and bounced its way into getting stuck between my bed frame and the floor. Unable to budge it, I pulled the bedcover over the ball. Surely, that's where it still was, and my need for denial was strong.

"Maybe you lost it," I offered.

Franklin shoved his hands in his pockets and stomped a foot. "I wanted to play with Earl," he said. Was I preventing that? I wondered. Did I have that power? He walked away disappointed, a sight that was not nearly as appealing as you might expect.

The confluence of my fear of discovery in an inappropriate game and the surprising guilt I felt at besting Franklin made the stakes of my deception seem much higher. I thought it advisable to find something else to do

46

before Franklin found his basketball in my room, so I told Pumpkin I was going to go visit the Manns for awhile.

"See you later," I said, patting her head good-bye. I walked quickly away.

Stepping onto the porch at the Manns' house, I reached for the doorbell. When Sylvia opened the door, she was wearing a large smock over elastic sweat pants. She still had some extra belly after having the baby.

"Hello, Hannah. How are you this afternoon?"

"I'm fine. Can I hold the baby?"

"I think so," she said. "Come on in. Ricky is just getting him up."

"Look at me, Hannah," Ricky said as he walked around the corner carrying the baby. "I'm a modern husband, changing diapers and everything. Next thing you know, I'll be cooking supper."

Sylvia smiled. "I can't wait to see that." She took Christopher and eased onto the couch. "Sit next to me, and you can hold him." As she unfolded her arms, she put Christopher into mine, and I held on tight.

"I tell you what," Ricky said, "we are glad to get this little boy, and he came right on time. He was floating up in heaven with all the other little babies, and when it was his time, he grabbed a parachute and came right on down. Got us on the front page of *The Wellton Courier*."

"I want to have a baby," I said, nodding.

47

Sylvia laughed. "Well, you'll have to wait for that until you get big."

"I know," I said. "I'll have to get really big. Like with the basketball under my shirt."

Somewhere in my mind, I was trying to confess my lie, but this quite naturally escaped the Manns' notice. As a practical matter, it's not that helpful to have your sins go undetected. If they do, you end up keeping them to yourself, and that's one of the hardest things there is.

Ricky reached in his shirt pocket for a cigarette. "Well, y'all enjoy your little visit. I'm going to step outside for some fresh air."

With the baby in my arms, I felt like a mother myself. I sat without speaking, but Christopher had something to say. His feet began to move, as if he were peddling a bicycle. Clinched fists started to swirl. With eyes squinted shut, his mouth formed into what seemed like a smile, but was really no smile at all. What followed was a sputtering sound that soon turned into a full-blown wail.

"He's telling us he's hungry," Sylvia said as she reached toward Christopher. "Here, let me take him."

"Yes, ma'am." I reluctantly returned her baby.

"Well, Hannah, it sure was nice to see you this afternoon," she said, standing with the baby. "We're glad you came by. Aren't we, Christopher?"

"Yes, ma'am," I said.

48

There are lots of ways to know to go home. Sometimes there's a specific signal—a whistle piercing the neighborhood, or the hum of a streetlight, or your mother's call. Or maybe it's something nonspecific, a vague sound or smell, that lets you remember you want to be home. And then there are those other times when the people whose home you are in begin to say things like, "It was so good to see you," or (like Sylvia), "We're glad you came by."

Soon after suppertime, I was sent to take my bath and put on my pajamas. As I hopped into bed, Daddy stepped in to say good night.

"Will you tell me a story?" I asked.

"Sure," he said as he sat beside me. "Once there was a little girl named Hannah." In Daddy's stories I was always the star. That's why I liked them. "She lived on the moon in a house in the shape of a sock, and she had lots of friends and a very special dog."

"Did she have a piano?" I asked.

"Yes, she had a beautiful piano, and each day when she played her beautiful piano, the sweet music was heard many miles away all over the earth."

"Was she sweet?"

"Oh, yes, she was a very sweet girl."

"Was she good?"

"Yes, she was a very good girl."

"Did she have any secrets?"

49

"Only the ones she did not want anyone to know." Daddy leaned over and kissed my forehead, then stood to leave. "Good night," he said, but I wanted him to stay longer.

"Daddy?"

"Yes?"

"Franklin's basketball is under my bed. It's stuck, and I can't get it out."

Daddy paused. "Wasn't he looking for it this afternoon?"

"Yes," I said, my voice quivering.

Daddy bent over and pulled the ball free.

"You can tell Franklin about it tomorrow."

"Would you tell him for me?"

"No, Hannah, I think you better tell him yourself. But if you want me to, I'll stand next to you when you do."

"Okay," I sighed. "I'll tell him."

SIX

umpkin was the family dog and liked us all, but I knew the one to whom she had given her heart. She fell hook, line, and sinker for Momma, largely due to Momma's indifference to her. Though I might yell all day long, "Here, Pumpkin. Here, girl," it was my mother to whom she responded—not to her calls, because Momma rarely called Pumpkin, but to her footsteps in the hallway.

Pumpkin stayed in overnight, often rotating from my bed to Franklin's, rolling off in the mornings when she heard Momma's slippers padding toward the kitchen. There's no doubt she knew who the momma was and that the household was in her care.

On Monday morning I felt the shift in weight on the bed when Pumpkin left my side and tapped her paw nails in Momma's direction. As the backdoor opened for Pumpkin to go out, I rolled over for more sleep. Momma's voice soon broke into my slumber. "Hannah, wake up," she said, nudging my shoulder. "Time to get up and get dressed."

Pulling myself out of bed, I reached for a dress laid on the chair and slipped it on. Stepping into saddle oxfords, I headed for the noisiness of the kitchen. Momma was frying

51

bacon; the sounds of the *Today Show* drifted in from the den; Daddy was at the table drinking coffee and reading the morning paper out loud.

"McGovern's a contender," he said, "but Wallace isn't out of the running."

"Black people won't vote for Wallace," Momma said.

"I don't suppose they will."

"Why won't black people vote for Wallace?" I asked as I walked through the doorway.

"Never mind," Momma explained. "I didn't see you standing there."

It was not like I was born yesterday. On the other hand, I had only been born seven years earlier, and I was unaware that George Wallace had used segregation of the races as a tool for political viability. Sadly, it was an effective calculation and one that would prove difficult to overcome, for others as well as himself. When you speak against someone, you can't always undo what was spoken.

Wallace was the governor of Alabama, campaigning that year for president. For all practical purposes, I couldn't tell the difference between Wallace and Richard Nixon. I mean that literally, not figuratively. On television, they looked a lot alike, and I couldn't tell them apart.

"Don't forget to feed Pumpkin," Momma said.

"Yes, ma'am." I retrieved a can of dog food from the pantry, pulled a chair to the counter, and crawled up to grab the can opener. Momma reached to open the backdoor.

"Let's see who's here this morning," she said.

Pumpkin had a lot of friends, and at daybreak they gathered near our kitchen like a Rotary Club for canines. Most were mutts—variations of collies, poodles, and beagles. Pumpkin was the only purebred in the bunch, but she never put on airs. She was just happy to see everybody.

When I pressed the handle down, the whirring of the can opener began, and Pumpkin rushed into the kitchen. Facing me, she lifted her front paws, trying to stand, then almost tripped me as I made my way to her bowl near the door. The food came out in one plop, still in the shape of a can, ridges and all.

As Pumpkin gobbled her food, I looked out the window and saw something which caused internal alarm bells to go off so loudly I'm surprised the sounds didn't escape through my ears: Ralph had joined the group. Ralph, a black, mostly Labrador mix, was what you might call a bad dog. He spent his days involved in petty dog crimes—barking at joggers and walkers, chasing cars, digging up gardens, and leaving unpleasant deposits on neighborhood lawns. There were also unsubstantiated allegations that he had murdered some kittens. Furthermore, Ralph wasn't from a good family. His people didn't go to church no matter how many times they got visited.

"What's Ralph doing here?" I asked Momma.

"I don't know," she said. "Maybe he followed the crowd."

"Can we keep Pumpkin inside today?"

"She wouldn't like that, Hannah. All her friends are outside."

My brow furrowed; there's no question I was worried. With Ralph around, I was afraid Pumpkin might fall in with the wrong crowd. Ralph seemed bad enough to be the wrong crowd all by himself.

I held such harsh judgment against this dog because I had seen what he was capable of. A free spirit, he tended to wander around all day, often in town. And he was a tempter. Once, he'd talked Pumpkin into going with him. Through my car window, I had seen them on the sidewalk near Earlie's Department Store, and I screamed to Momma, "There's Pumpkin!"

"Well, my word," she said, veering into a nearby parking place. I opened my door and called to Pumpkin. Eagerly, she jumped into the car.

"What were you thinking?" I asked as I held her close. "You're too far away."

Free spirits leave home. That much I knew. That is not what I wanted for my special friend. And now the tempter, Ralph, had found his way into my own backyard.

"I'd better go check on Franklin." Momma placed my breakfast on the table and turned toward the hallway. Franklin was always getting checked on because his habits of punctuality were inconsistent. He was as slow as Christmas when it came time to getting ready for school.

54

But when it came time to bothering me or touching my stuff without my permission, he was as quick as could be. On that matter, perhaps, our score was even. I did apologize over the basketball, but I felt a little strange about it. I'd never said anything like that to Franklin, and even with Daddy standing there, it seemed to change something between us. We established a truce of sorts, if only a temporary one.

Pumpkin finished her last few bites, eased her way under the table, and rested near my feet. From my chair I could see Ralph and the other dogs in the backyard.

"Daddy, can we keep Ralph out of our yard?"

"I don't see how," he said. He folded his newspaper and took a sip of coffee.

"We can build a fence."

"Fences aren't very neighborly, Hannah."

I didn't know what to say to that, but I tried to think of something. All through my breakfast, I mulled over a response to "Fences aren't very neighborly." Finally, as Daddy got up from the table, took his dishes to the sink, and stepped into the hallway, I had the answer.

"Being a bad dog isn't very neighborly either," I said. No response from Daddy meant that he didn't hear me. Not wanting to waste my good comeback, I pushed my chair from the table and ran after him. While I looked for Daddy in the back of the house, I heard our wooden front door scrape against the door frame; he stepped outside, walked down the concrete steps, and headed to his car. I ran into the living room and pulled the door open as Daddy slammed his car door shut and revved the engine. He gave a little wave when he saw me standing in the driveway, then he backed into the street, straightened his car, and accelerated toward the corner. I gave a little wave back and watched until he took the turn and was no longer in sight. I would have to tell him later.

"Franklin!" Momma called as I walked back into the house. "It's time to go."

Her call was followed by the sound of several things falling to the floor. A moment later Franklin appeared in the doorway of the living room. "I'm ready," he said.

"What happened back there?" Momma asked.

"My books fell off the night stand."

"Did anything break?"

"No, ma'am."

"How did they fall?"

"I knocked them off by accident."

"How did you knock them off?"

"I tripped as I was trying to grab them."

"Are your shoes tied?"

"They are now."

"Alright," Momma said, "let's go or we'll be late."

Soon, we were backing out of the driveway in Momma's car, a silver version of Daddy's brown one. At

56

the corner, Momma slammed on the brakes as she prepared to turn right onto Southview.

"My gracious!" she said.

From the backseat, I half-stood and leaned toward the front. "What happened?"

"Mr. Stevens almost ran into us as he was turning onto our street."

"He cut too sharp," Franklin said.

"Sharply," Momma corrected. "Mr. Stevens cut too sharply."

I was a little disappointed that we hadn't actually wrecked our car. That could have given me a great deal to talk about in school, and, plus, maybe I would have gotten to use crutches for a broken foot, assuming I had actually broken a foot if we had actually had a wreck. It just wasn't my lucky day.

As we continued, I leaned against the backseat, sinking as far down as possible, watching treetops along Southview pass by my window. From that angle I couldn't see the houses. Only the trees could tell me where I was. I kind of had the idea that if I were ever trying to find my way home from the perspective of a magic carpet, or a helicopter, or a little plane, I might need to have the trees memorized. And if my whole family were trying to make it home from the perspective of a magic carpet, or a helicopter, or a little plane, I would be the only one to have had the forethought to memorize the trees, and I would be the hero.

Memorizing the trees along Southview wasn't as easy as you might think. The only one I knew for sure was a large oak standing at the corner of Southview and Earlie. When the tall, green-leaved limbs cast a shadow over our car, I popped my head up and watched the rest of the scenery from my level window.

A short time later Momma pulled up to the front of the school and let us out. "I'll see you at the church after choir, okay?" On Monday afternoons, Franklin and I walked from the school to choir practice at the church, and that's where Momma picked us up when we were done.

"Yes, ma'am," we both said, gathering our books. "See you then."

Franklin slammed the front door and turned toward the school. I slammed the backdoor, but waited at the curb to wave at Momma's car as she drove away. I followed it with my eyes to the bottom of hill, and then it turned left to go back home.

seven

·:◉:·

S ome smells are profound, like the odor of red
granules on a tile school floor in a musty hallway
mixed with the vomit of a first grader. This is what
I got a whiff of as I came near my room. The bell rang and
the hallway cleared, except for old Mr. Burns, the janitor,
who was stooped over a large broom and muttering as he
swept, "Don't know why children have to vomit in school.
Don't need to eat breakfast if they're just going to vomit it
right on my clean floor."

Passing through the congestion of first graders in the
doorway, I took a seat in my desk at the front of the classroom.
Emily Jeffers poked me on the shoulder from behind.

"Arnold Johnson threw up," she whispered.

"Ewww . . . ," I said. Many times I have been content
in my judgment of others, and this was one of those times.
That Arnold Johnson was undesirable had been decided
early in the year, the benefit for the rest of us being a standing
recess game: tagging another and saying, "You've got
Arnold Johnson's germs." He was dirty and picked his nose
and now he'd vomited in school.

The circumstance of birth had made Arnold different,
and our response to him was based on a simple notion: to

59

be born in lesser circumstances made him less worthy. It was easy not to think of him as a real boy with hopes and fears. I thought of him instead as a school yard game that I didn't want to lose.

"Okay, class," Mrs. Simpson said from her desk, "settle down and let me call the roll."

Two things I remember specifically about my first grade teacher, the first being that Mrs. Simpson was thirty-one years old. At some point in the year when one of the students asked her how old she was, she answered the question, and that piece of information has been stored in my brain ever since. The other thing particular to Mrs. Simpson is that she was of another race. The city schools had integrated a couple of years before, and Mrs. Simpson was one of the first black teachers at Wellton Elementary. Everything else about her is a little hazy, except that I'm sure I loved her like I would have loved anyone who taught me. Loving the teacher, and taking for granted that the teacher loved me, was a part of my make up.

On Mondays and Wednesdays, Mrs. Simpson taught us reading, then escorted us to music class in the auditorium. The school had no music studio. We marched single file to folding chairs set up in a semicircle on the auditorium stage. A music stand was in the center of the circle, with an upright piano to the side. The piano wasn't a pretty one. The ivory had worn off some of the keys, exposing the wood. Over the years students had scratched messages on the back of the

60

piano. Someone had scratched "Lisa loves Bill." Right beneath, another had scratched "Jesus loves you."

Mrs. Lloyd had been the music teacher for most of the year, during which her belly kept getting larger and larger. In February and March I had watched from my chair as she grew less and less comfortable on the piano bench. She seemed also to increase in crankiness. After spring break she quit coming to school at all; instead she went to the hospital to have a baby, and on this Monday music class got a new teacher, Evelyn Myers.

"Good morning, class," Miss Myers said cheerfully as we each settled into our chairs. Standing in front of us at the music stand, she was wearing the prettiest clothes I had ever seen—a cream-colored linen jacket and slacks, with a mustard-yellow silk blouse and brown suede shoes. A silk scarf tied around her neck had browns and yellows with a little bit of mauve, all accented by thick, brown hair pulled tight into a clip.

"Does anyone know how to play the piano?" she asked the class. My hand shot high into the air.

"That's wonderful," she said. "You're Hannah Hayes, aren't you?"

"Yes, ma'am," I said.

Miss Myers lived with her parents on Earlie, just a few houses down from the large oak tree, and I had seen her before. Besides, it was never a surprise to me when someone knew my name. I expected it.

61

"Well, Hannah Hayes," she continued, "why don't you come sit with me on the piano bench?"

I jumped from my chair and, in doing so, accidentally kicked one of the chair's legs, which caused me to teeter momentarily, but I caught my balance and stayed upright long enough to join Miss Myers at the piano.

"Can you play something for us?" she asked when I took my seat next to her.

"Yes, ma'am." I played a five-note, one-fingered melody my mother had taught me.

"Very nice. Have you taken lessons?"

"No, ma'am. I will next year."

"Well, that is wonderful. Now, I need a little help here, if you don't mind. Do you think you could be my page turner?"

"Yes, ma'am," I said.

"My hands are so busy on the piano keys," Miss Myers explained, "that I need a third hand to turn the pages at the appropriate time. It's unfortunate that I only have two hands, but I'll have to do the best I can and let you do the rest."

"Yes, ma'am," I said.

I sat at the piano bench with Miss Myers for the rest of the class period, turning the pages whenever she nodded. It was hard for my little fingers to grab a single sheet. Sometimes I turned two or three pages at a time. Miss Myers never minded; she brushed the extras back and kept playing.

"Thanks for helping me, Hannah Hayes," Miss Myers said when the class was over.

"You're welcome," I said as she patted me on the back.

Near the end of the day, my classmates and I were silently working on our letters when Mrs. Simpson spoke from her desk. "Who's humming?" she asked. Her question startled me and I looked around the room.

"It's Hannah," Emily Jeffers said.

"Hannah," Mrs. Simpson said, "stop humming."

Had it been me? This was not the first time this had happened. Mrs. Simpson would stop the class, ask who was humming, and Emily Jeffers would say, "It's Hannah." I was dismayed to be told on, but Emily was just that way. She kept a watchful eye.

Soon the bell rang, school was out for the day, and I met up with Franklin at the front door. We started down a long hill and then went up a long hill leading to the church. Our choir practices, separated by age groups, lasted about an hour, then Momma came to retrieve us at the overhang in the parking lot. On this Monday after choir, she dropped Franklin and me off at home but stayed in the car.

"I've got to run a quick errand," she explained. "I'll be back in a minute."

Franklin and I trudged into the house without any particular interest in one other. Entering my room, I threw my books on the bed and pulled off my clothes. Pausing, I

63

sniffed the school's odors on the fabric of my dress. Everywhere I went during the day, the odors of the school attached to my clothes, and I took home small whiffs of the classrooms, the playground, the auditorium, and the lunch-room. I never noticed the smells during the day, only later when I discarded my outfit.

From the kitchen, I heard Pumpkin tapping on the linoleum, and I hurried to catch up. Grabbing shorts and a T-shirt from a drawer, I dressed quickly. The sound moved toward the living room and I followed, finding Pumpkin in one of her favorite places, a cool spot under the sofa. Lying on the floor, face to face with Pumpkin, I called her name. She offered only a blink of her eyes in response.

Standing, my short attention span was diverted by the piano. I sat on the bench and placed my right forefinger on middle C. Pressing down, I held it for four counts. It was a fine sound; I pressed the key next to it for another four counts. I was about to press the key next to that one when a shadow fell across the piano. Franklin was watching. He stood beside me in shorts, no shirt. He was barefoot, and his straight brown hair was going in all directions. He never did have much use for combs.

"What are you doing?" he asked.

"I'm playing the piano."

"No, you're not. You don't know how to play the piano."

64

"You are so silly, Franklin. Do you see me pressing the key? I am playing the piano."

"You know why Miss Myers wanted you to be her page turner, don't you?"

"Because she needed me," I said.

Franklin had a spy in my classroom, but I did not know who it was. He had a way of knowing things that had taken place. One time he found out the name of a classmate who was, bless his heart, a fat, unattractive boy. Franklin used to tease me with, "Hannah loves Thomas Sims," only for the purpose of creating wholesale panic within my soul.

"You're the page turner," Franklin said, "because you can't play the piano."

"That's not true!" I was stung by the accusation.

When Franklin left the room, I began to breathe easier—until his return a few moments later. He held in his hands a pinwheel, a rubber band, and a box of matches. He picked up a candlestick from a nearby coffee table, repositioned the candle in the holder, and leaned it against the music rack on the piano.

"What are you doing?" I asked.

"I'm inventing an automatic page turner," he said.

Franklin took the rubber band and wrapped it around the candlestick and pinwheel. The idea was that the heat from the candle would cause the pinwheel to spin and the spinning pinwheel would cause the pages to turn. But when he struck a match and lit the candle, wax dripped on the

65

piano and the plastic stick of the pinwheel started to melt, which caused the pinwheel's fan to droop.

"You're making a mess!" I yelled.

"That's because I'm inventing something," he said. According to Franklin's logic, if you're inventing something, it doesn't matter if you make a mess. The fact that you make a mess is canceled out by the good you're doing for society.

Franklin left all that stuff on the piano and stormed out of the room. I was immobilized by the debris and didn't know what to clean up first, but it was of no matter: Franklin returned with an oscillating fan which he stationed on top of the piano, pointing downward. When he plugged the fan in the wall socket and flipped it on, sheets of music blew everywhere.

"Franklin," I screamed, "you're making an awful mess!"

"It's turning the pages," he said triumphantly.

The front door scraped against the door frame; Daddy was home. "Hi, kids. What's going on in here?" he asked.

"Franklin's making a mess," I said.

"I'm inventing a page turner," Franklin protested.

"Oh, I see," Daddy said. He walked to the piano, glancing at the melted structure. "Franklin, are you sure you're not reinventing the pinwheel?"

Daddy had made a joke, but it went over our heads, and we looked at him like he was some old man who didn't know what he was talking about. A moment later Momma came through the front door herself. When she saw the mess, was she ever mad at Franklin.

"I can't take my eyes off either of you for a minute," she said. "Both of you, clean this mess up and go to your rooms."

"But Momma!" we protested simultaneously.

"I've told you not to play in the living room."

"Better do what she says, kids," Daddy intervened. "I'll get this part." He gingerly picked up the pinwheel and candlestick, while I picked up papers from the floor and put them back on the music rack. Franklin grabbed the fan and put it in the hall closet as he headed toward his room. I left too, looking back once at Momma to see if she had realized her mistake about my complete innocence in this matter. Her hands on her hips and her grim look let me know that she was still unaware of which one of us had been truly in the wrong. I let it go.

"It sure is fun to come home to a war zone," Daddy was saying to Momma as I walked out.

"One more crack like that and you're going to *your* room."

"Well, I wouldn't mind going to my room if you were going too," he said.

"Oh, hush," was the last thing I heard as I closed my bedroom door and began my suffering in silence.

For a long while, sitting on my bed, I had an opportunity to reflect on the injustice of the situation. The rule was

67

"no playing in the living room." Technically, I had not broken the rule because, technically, I had not been playing. Sure, the word "playing" was involved, as in playing the piano, but it was not playing in the traditional sense, as in playing with Barbie dolls. Franklin was the one who turned it into playing, and he was the one who made the mess.

Hours later, or what seemed like hours but may have only been fifteen minutes, Daddy let us out of our jails.

"Supper's almost ready," he said as he poked his head in my room. "Go wash up."

Franklin and I ran to the bathroom and pushed and shoved our way through the nightly ritual to prepare our hands for dinner.

"Franklin, you're splashing me," I said.

"Move over," he said.

We each grabbed an end of a towel, wiped our hands dry, and rushed side by side into the kitchen, where we found Momma handing plates filled with food to Daddy, who put them on the table. "Franklin, get some napkins," Momma said. "And, Hannah, get the salt and pepper shakers."

When we were all seated at the kitchen table, Daddy said a quick blessing. "Dear Lord, bless this food for the nourishment of our bodies and bless our bodies for Thy service. Amen." I opened my eyes, looked down at my plate, and was immediately overcome by the threat of several tiny trees.

"I don't like broccoli," I complained.

"Yes, you do," Momma said. "You love broccoli. Remember when you had broccoli at Grandmother Louise's?"

"I remember."

"You liked it then; you'll like it now."

"I don't like ham," Franklin said.

"Life is not all French fries," Daddy interrupted. "Into every life, some ham must fall."

"Life is not all French fries, Franklin," I repeated. I bravely took a bite of broccoli, as we each settled in to the meal before us. The only sound was the clinking of forks against the plates until Momma broke the silence.

"How'd your meeting go?" she asked Daddy.

"I guess okay," he shrugged. "Tom's been reading in all his 'How to be a CEO' magazines that corporate social responsibility is the big thing these days, so he wants me to come up with some ideas on how to let people know we're a socially responsible corporation. He wants to be seen as a leader in responsible living."

"That sounds important," Momma said.

"Yes, very important, so I asked him if he believed that the company was a responsible corporate citizen. And he said, 'I'm shocked you should ask such a question. Hamilton Sock Company is for God, country, and family— it always has been, and it's going to stay that way as long as I have anything to do with it.'"

"That's responsible," Momma said.

69

"Yes, very responsible, so I explained, 'I wasn't asking the question because I didn't believe it was true, but because I wanted to know your view on the matter.' So he explained, 'Everybody today is for the environment, right? At Hamilton Sock Company, we are for the environment. We're against litter, aren't we? We have trash cans everywhere, don't we? Let's put some signs on them that say 'Hamilton Sock Company is against litter.'"

Daddy cut into his ham and took a bite. "So I said, 'That will certainly send them a message. But we can't just be against something. We have to be *for* something, don't we? And Tom said, 'I told you, we are for God, country, and family.'"

"I'm for God, country, and family, Daddy," Franklin said.

"I am too, Daddy," I said.

"Me too," Momma said.

"Thank you, one and all. It's good to have you on our side."

A few moments passed until Momma broke the silence again. "Remember, don't feed Pumpkin from the table," she said to no one in particular. Three hands—one of Franklin's, one of Daddy's, and one of mine—quickly returned to three laps.

eight

⊙

I t occurs to me now that, in matters of religion, the larger groups are defined by a common concept: we're right, they're wrong. That's called a faith. In the case of Christianity, each group narrows into smaller groups defined by the same concept: we're right, they're wrong. That's called a denomination.

Like many a good believer, I was already picking up on these differences—not the exact differences, just that there were differences and that whatever I believed was right and whatever anyone else believed (if different) was wrong. I remember that as we drove past other congregations on Sunday mornings, I would watch people enter their own sanctuaries and wonder to myself why they didn't know they were going to the wrong church.

The Jehovah's Witnesses were trying to bring others into their fold. When members were seen knocking on doors in the neighborhoods, their proselytizing prompted phone call advisories. That's how we knew on Saturday afternoon that they were headed our way.

"If you answer the door when they come," Momma said to me, "you are to be polite, but don't let them inside. If you let them inside, we won't be able to get them out."

As she spoke, I was trying to picture in my mind the kind of situation that would lead to the phrase "we won't be able to get them out." Maybe something happened to Jehovah's Witnesses when they entered the home of Baptists, something like an allergic reaction. Maybe they blew up like balloons and were no longer able to fit through the front door. Or maybe they were too fast, like Pumpkin sometimes was, and they ran and hid under the sofa.

Shortly, the Jehovah's Witnesses rang the bell, and I pulled open the front door to be greeted by a man and a woman, both of whom were wearing their Sunday clothes on a Saturday.

"Hello," they said.

"Hello," I said.

"How are you today?" the man asked.

"I'm not supposed to let you inside," I said.

"That's okay," the woman responded. "We'll stay outside. Are your parents home?"

"I'm not supposed to tell you that."

"We understand," the man said. "Do you have a church that you go to?"

"Of course I go to church." I couldn't believe he would ask such a silly question. Didn't I look like a churchgoer? Didn't this house look like a home for churchgoers?

"We want to leave this information for you and your parents," the woman said as she handed me a leaflet. "If you or your parents have any questions, I hope you'll let us know."

72

Momma was behind me by then, drawing the door closed that I had opened wide. "Thank you for stopping by," she said. "But we have a church already."

"Oh, you're home." The woman smiled at my mother.

"Thank you for stopping by," Momma repeated. "We have a church already." She almost had the door shut when Pumpkin came sneaking up behind us, seeking escape. Momma caught her by the collar and raised her other hand to the doorknob.

"Thank you for stopping by," Momma said again. As she closed the door and let go of Pumpkin, I tried to digest what had happened.

"Why did they come by?" I asked.

"They want to bring others into their fold," she said.

"What's a fold?"

"It's a group of people, like a church."

"Like our church?"

"Well, not exactly," Momma said. "Theirs is different from our church." She turned to walk toward the kitchen, and I followed.

"Why don't they just come to our church?"

"They want to go to their own church, and they want other people to go with them. All churches want more people."

An important principle was unfolding: you can't be a fold all by yourself. To be a fold, you've got to get someone else in there with you.

73

"It's a beautiful day," Momma said as she pulled open the kitchen window. "Why don't you see if Sammy is home? Or why don't you call Debbie? Franklin's outside playing. You should be outside too."

"I want to play the piano. Will you teach me another song?"

"I've taught you all the songs I know already. We'll have to find you a real piano teacher for next year if you want to learn more. But right now you should be playing outside. It's too pretty to be inside. Go outside and ride your bike." At Momma's prodding, I was soon out the backdoor, waiting for next year to learn a new song.

I liked my bike because it had a pretty blue and white banana seat. But I didn't always like riding it, especially among the small hills on Southview. The on and off process was an unsatisfactory mix of riding downhill and pushing uphill.

The riding I kept to my street, and most often it was reduced to the short hop to Sammy's. I moved toward the side of the house where I'd parked my bike, then pulled myself onto the banana seat. Lifting the kick stand, I headed for Sammy's. When I rang the bell, his mother answered.

"Well, hello, Hannah."

"Hi, Mrs. Morris. Can Sammy come out and play?"

"I suppose for a little while," she said. Sammy poked his head around his mother's waist. "Do you want to go

74

outside and play for a little while?" she asked him. "Don't get too dirty now."

Sammy stepped through the door wearing cowboy boots, shorts, and a pajama top with a cowboy print. "That's a pajama top," I exclaimed. I knew that, as a general rule, you weren't supposed to go outside in the middle of the day wearing a pajama top. Sammy was clearly violating this standard of good raising.

"It's a cowboy shirt," he said. "I'm a cowboy."

"But it's really a pajama top."

"I'm a cowboy," he said.

I was about to explain again to Sammy that he was wearing a pajama top outside and in the daytime when Mrs. Morris interrupted. "Sammy's pretending to be a cowboy today," she said. That left no room for argument.

"Do you want to ride bikes?" I asked Sammy.

Mrs. Morris took the question. "Sammy's still on training wheels, you know. Maybe y'all can play in the driveway or the vacant lot. Just stay near the house."

Mrs. Morris watched us walk toward the lot next door. "I'll come check on y'all in a little while," she said, then stepped back inside. Moments later, as I glanced toward the kitchen window, Mrs. Morris was twisting the blinds open.

When Sammy and I settled in the lot, we realized that the hole we had begun to China showed barely a dent. Traveling to foreign lands was not quite right for the day anyway.

A plastic dump truck, fire truck, and eighteen-wheeler were in the lot from one of Sammy's earlier play times. When we picked them up, we instinctively knew to start crashing them into what would now be our ditch. I give Sammy credit for this: he was good with sound effects. He could make things screech, collide, or implode with a few, carefully crafted noises.

After awhile, we thought it might be more fun to crash vehicles into a pond instead of a ditch, so Sammy ran to the back of his house, running water from the faucet into a nearby watering bucket. I followed, and it's a good thing, because it took both of us to carry the water bucket and pour it into our ditch.

When one bucket of water made a small pond, we couldn't think of any reason not to make it bigger. We were off for a second bucket, then a third. By then it made more sense to stretch the garden hose as far as it would go and spray the dry land around us. That the land had turned to mud was fine with us until Sammy stepped too close to our pond; the suction of the mud captured his boots.

"My boots won't walk," he said, agitated and teetering for balance.

"Let's pretend you're in quicksand," I offered helpfully.

"But my boots won't walk," he said again, near tears. When I stepped closer to pull him out, my tennis shoes were caught in the mud's suction. Quickly I stepped back; my feet came with me, but my shoes stayed in the mud.

76

"I can't get out of the quicksand!" he said in full panic.

I looked toward the house as Sammy's mother reappeared in the kitchen window. In the next instant, she was out the front door. This particular combination—the fact that his mother was advancing urgently and he couldn't move—was enough to start Sammy crying.

"Look at what a mess you are," she said as she took his arms and lifted him out of his boots. Setting him on the driveway, she swatted his behind. For good measure, I suppose, she turned and swatted mine too.

"Y'all know better than to drag all this water out here. My gracious."

My eyes turned hot with held-back tears. Being swatted on the behind by a neighbor was a terrible reflection on my belief in my own popularity, and I could barely speak. Mumbling "I have to go home now," I dragged my shoes out of the mud and lifted the kick stand on my bike. Because my shoes were too muddy to wear, and because I couldn't steer the handlebars and hold the shoes, I pushed my bike all the way home.

At the backdoor, I washed my feet beneath an outside faucet and left my shoes on the steps. When I walked inside, Daddy was watching golf in the den, and Momma was sitting in there too.

"I need to run and go get a few things for supper," she said, standing. "What are you about to do, Hannah?"

"I'm going to play in my room now."

"Okay, then, I'll see you in a little while."

I walked into my room and fell on my bed, still exasperated about my experiences at the Morrises. The front door opened and closed as Momma left for the store, and the sound of paws came down the hallway.

"Here, Pumpkin," I called. "Here, girl." She jumped up to join me. While I stroked her back, our four eyelids grew heavy. I was sound asleep when I felt Momma jostle me.

"Hannah, get up. Come on into the kitchen and let's eat." Disoriented, I shook off the sleep and rose from my bed.

"What's for breakfast?" I asked as I walked into the kitchen.

"Breakfast!" Franklin howled. "It's not breakfast time. It's suppertime!"

"Rip Van Hannah must think she was asleep for a long time," Daddy said.

Was it not morning? When I looked down, I wasn't wearing pajamas. I was wearing the same shorts and shirt I had worn to the Morrises. Was it nighttime? Slowly, I remembered. Pumpkin and I had a nap. Now back in the right time and place, I took a seat at the table, put my napkin in my lap, ate my beans and carrots without being prompted, said "please" when I asked for the biscuits and "thank you" when they came my way.

When it was bedtime, I wasn't at all sleepy. In hopes of extending this curfew, I asked Momma to tell me a story.

Rather than making one up, like Daddy usually did, she opted for the storybook on my bedside table.

"What will it be tonight?" she asked.

"The Shoemaker and the Elves."

"Alright. That's a good one." Momma began to read this Grimm Brothers' tale about a poor shoemaker and his wife. Each night the shoemaker laid out materials that he would use to make shoes the next morning. Each morning, he found that during the night his work had already been completed. This was so puzzling that one night the shoemaker and his wife stayed up to spy on whoever was doing their work, and it turned out to be two naked elves. Because the elves had made them rich, the shoemaker and his wife made each one a nice set of clothes in repayment. The next night when the elves came in and saw their new clothes, they dressed happily, danced around, and left.

I always liked that story, though I haven't found its lessons to be true. The work laid out for me couldn't be done by another. A call can only be answered by the one called.

In my view, you have to be careful about the stories you accept without question. People can tell you all sorts of things that could prove contrary to what is in your heart and your mind. Until you know what those things are, you can find yourself all in a dither trying to please someone simply because he's the one speaking out. Or she is, rather.

That reminds me of a story my mother never liked to hear. Martha Holmes, a friend of Momma's, had called her to tell how nervous she was about upcoming cheerleader tryouts for her daughter Cindy. Cindy had tried out twice in junior high school, but did not make the cheerleader team either time, and now she was giving it one more shot. Mrs. Holmes was expressing her fear that Cindy might not make the team again. If she didn't, it would be the third straight year of rejection, and that's tough on a parent.

Momma listened sympathetically, and in an inspired moment said, "I'll add Cindy to our prayer chain." But when Momma placed the call to Mrs. Hamilton, the first person on the chain, she got an unexpected response.

"We don't pray for cheerleader tryouts," Mrs. Hamilton explained. "That is vanity."

Momma was wounded that a prayer request had been rebuffed, guilt-ridden that she was not able to provide this assistance to her friend, and confused about whether or not she had tried to use the prayer chain inappropriately.

"I didn't realize Myra Hamilton's prayer chain had bylaws," Daddy said when Momma told him. "What is it okay to pray for, if not cheerleaders? A winning football team? A good day in the stock market?"

Momma's reply was empty of spirit. "I think she favors world peace," she said.

It was a simple incident, but it made Momma self-conscious about asking for prayer. And that's exactly what you have to be careful about—letting someone else interfere in your communion with God, even if done with good intentions.

I don't remember Momma calling Myra Hamilton that day, but I do remember hearing about it. It happened only a few months after Tom Hamilton's Uncle Andrew had died and he had become company president.

Andrew was the one who had made my father the marketing and public relations manager, but his ways of generating publicity weren't in keeping with standard practice. He once received a Driving While Intoxicated citation while behind the wheel of a golf cart. He'd been on his way back from the course to the company when his weaving maneuvers caught the attention of a police officer, and a photograph of the incident made its way to the front page of *The Wellton Courier*. But the publicity didn't seem to have an ill effect on the company. As Andrew liked to tell my father, "Socks sell, Martin. It's as simple as that."

nine

School mornings had a synchronized pattern, with each participant playing a different role: Momma prepared breakfast, Daddy read the paper out loud, I fed Pumpkin, and Franklin ran late. Jumping out of bed was harder for Franklin than it was for me. That's probably why I was Pumpkin's feeder. A task goes to the one most ready to assume it.

"Good morning, bright eyes," Daddy said as I walked into the kitchen. He poured a cup of coffee from the pot on the counter and took it to the table. Following my own routine, I retrieved a can of dog food from the pantry, pulled a chair to the counter, and crawled up to grab the can opener.

"Let's see who's here this morning," Momma said, reaching for the door. Stepping off the chair, I plopped Pumpkin's food in her bowl and dropped the empty container in the trash can. When Pumpkin ran in for breakfast, I looked out to the patio. Ralph had shown up for many mornings, and he was here again. Disappointed, I took my seat at the table.

"Wallace is taking a trip," Daddy said as he spread out his paper. "He'll be gone for four weeks."

"My gracious. Where's he going?" Momma asked. She set a bowl of oatmeal in front of me.

"Up North, running for president."

"Why would he go up there when he lives here?" I asked.

"A lot of people are asking that very question, Hannah," Daddy answered without looking from his paper. "Why would he go up there running for president when he ought to be down here running the state? A lot of people are asking that."

I felt proud to be asking the very question that a lot of people were asking. I followed up by turning my question into a statement. "He ought not be going up there if he lives down here," I said, shaking my head in disapproval. It seemed a simple matter to me that, if you had something important to do, you ought to do it at home.

Daddy wiped his mouth with his napkin and pushed his chair back. "I've got to run. See y'all at suppertime."

"See you at suppertime, Daddy."

After breakfast Momma sent me to brush my teeth, and I had fully intended to do just that but got sidetracked by my image in the bathroom mirror. Speaking into a hairbrush, I announced, "And now, ladies and gentlemen, we are very lucky to have with us this morning the big star, Hannah Hayes."

Momma popped her head into the bathroom with a reminder. "Someone's going to be very unlucky this morning if she doesn't brush her teeth and get ready for school."

"Yes, ma'am," I sighed, squeezing toothpaste onto my toothbrush. Still it was hard to concentrate, even as I brushed. I hummed along to the fantasies in my head that had me on a stage in a room full of people, singing at the top of my lungs. But even a big star has to stop to spit and rinse.

Nothing went well that morning in school. Mrs. Simpson said my letters weren't neat and that I needed to be more careful. And when she asked who wanted to take the attendance chart to the school office, she picked Emily Jeffers instead of me. Overcome by disappointment, I rushed to get to the head of the single-file line when it was time for music class.

"Slow down, Hannah," Mrs. Simpson said. But I wasn't running, not technically. I was only walking fast. Even so, I was sent to the end of the line and was the last, the very last, to get to the auditorium.

The minute I spotted Miss Myers, I asked her, "Can I sit next to you and turn the pages?"

"I suppose that would be okay," she said. I started to relax. No one had asked her before I got there, so I sat next to her again, turning the pages whenever she nodded. I loved to watch her hands as she played. They moved like magic across the keys.

"How do you get your hands to play like that?" I asked her at the end of class.

84

"It doesn't come from my hands," she said. "It comes from my head and my heart. My hands follow their lead."

"Oh," I said.

Miss Myers removed sheets of music from the piano's rack, while my classmates began to line up to file out. "If I were going to be here next year, you could have taken piano lessons from me, but I'm probably moving to Birmingham."

"Why would you move to Birmingham?" I asked.

"Well," she shrugged as she stood, "I have a boyfriend there."

The word "boyfriend" made Miss Myers smile, which caused me to put my hand over my mouth and giggle. When you're in first grade, boyfriend is a very funny word. Can you imagine how easy it would be to become a stand-up comedian for first graders? You'd only have to stand in front of a classroom and say, "Miss Myers has a *boyfriend*," and the whole class would crack up.

My giggles prompted a few giggles from Miss Myers herself. "You are so silly," she said as she patted my head.

Toward the end of the day I sat in my desk working on my letters, until I was distracted by a question from Mrs. Simpson. "Who's humming?" she asked from her desk. I looked around to see who was humming.

"It's Hannah," Emily Jeffers said.

"Hannah, stop humming."

85

"Yes, ma'am."

But I really didn't know how to stop humming. It's not like it came from my mouth or my nose. Like Miss Myers said—music came from my head and my heart, and there was nothing I could do to hold it in.

When the school bell rang, I was glad to be free. I met up with Franklin in the front of the building, and we walked to the church for choir practice. Franklin hadn't had much to say to me the whole way there, and I hadn't had much to say to him. Until, that is, we reached the church. As we stepped through the door, Franklin said a horrible thing: "You love Arnold Johnson."

"I don't either!" I yelled. "Take it back!" My voice reverberated through the empty hallway just as Miss Carter, the church secretary, walked by.

"Hannah Hayes," she chastised, "we do not yell in the Lord's house."

"Yes, ma'am."

+ e ^

*A*ll week long Ralph had congregated with Pumpkin and her friends, and once again I had seen the direct result of Ralph's bad influence when, on the ride home from school, I discovered Pumpkin following him down Earlie Street. Disturbed, I decided that I needed to have a long talk with Pumpkin to explain to her the errors of her ways and set her on the path to the straight and narrow. Thus on Saturday afternoon, hearing a preacher's clear call to restore a friend to a more faithful walk, I delivered my first sermon from the piano bench in our living room.

Rummaging through my closet, I grabbed an old dress and walked through the house calling for Pumpkin. She didn't answer, but I found her anyway, resting underneath the living room sofa. As I peered under the sofa, face to face, eye-to-eye, she slowly stretched and eased out.

"Time for church," I said. Pumpkin sat with her head down while I pulled the neck of the dress over her head. Climbing onto the piano bench, I began to preach.

"And the Word says, let us not be bad children but let us be good children," I announced. "Let us mind our manners at all times and not be selfish or lazy. Let us put

87

away our toys when we are done and let us not be messy. Praise be the name of the Lord.

"Now, I want to talk to the lost souls," I continued as I hopped off the bench. "Pumpkin, are you being a good dog? If you do something when we can't see you, will we still be proud of you?" I felt fully in the spirit, until I sensed that Franklin was in the room.

"What are you doing?" he asked.

"I'm preaching to the lost souls."

Franklin nodded, then reached down to pull the dress over Pumpkin's neck. "Robert Phillips is going to be a preacher. He's getting ordained tomorrow night."

"What's ordained?"

Franklin handed me the dress, ignoring my question. Pumpkin had been waiting patiently for the church service to resume, but, bored by the delay, began a slow exit from the living room. She crouched, as if she did not wish to disturb our conversation; her nails tapped on the hardwood floor.

"Pumpkin!" I yelled. Her speed increased, and she was quickly out of sight.

"You shouldn't put a dress on Pumpkin," Franklin said. "She doesn't like it."

"It's important to wear our good clothes in the house of the Lord," I replied. "We are showing our respect."

The bad thing about Franklin coming into the living room was not only the part about him bothering me, but he also had a way of getting us banished.

"Kids, I don't want you playing in here," Momma said as she poked her head in from the kitchen. "Why don't you run outside and play?"

"But Momma . . . ," I said.

"Get some fresh air," she interrupted. "Go do something. And what are you doing with that dress?"

"I'm going to the Fords," Franklin said as he yanked the front door open.

"Hannah, go see if you can find someone to play with too." Momma gave me a little push onto the porch as she took the dress from my hands. Franklin, quickly peddling his bicycle, was far ahead of me, and Pumpkin, having also been pushed out by Momma, was a few steps behind. When I turned to talk to Pumpkin, she was already in pursuit of an unknown scent and sniffed her way out of sight.

Franklin and I didn't have the same boundaries. The confines of my world were all of Evergreen, a right-angle turn onto Southview, and all backyards along the way. I wasn't allowed past the Morgans' house, where Southview met Earlie at the end of that right angle. Franklin could ride his bike to town straight down Earlie, and he could also take a left on Southview and go up the other direction. This wasn't fair, but when you're seven, what can you do? I

89

had been petitioning for extensions to my boundary, but so far, my parents weren't budging.

"I don't want you anywhere outside the range of my voice," Momma had said. "When I call you to come home, I want you to be able to hear me."

My urge to preach had not yet subsided, and so I began to canvass the neighborhood in search of other dogs who needed to hear about the error of their ways. I walked toward the end of my street and took a right onto the sidewalk on Southview. For a moment, I considered stopping to see Debbie Sellers. Though her house was only a few houses down from mine, it faced Southview and was on a slight incline. Looking up at the steep driveway, I thought better of putting the energy into the climb and continued my walk. Besides, what was the point of playing with Debbie Sellers? Pale and fragile, she would just as soon stay inside and read a book.

The sidewalk curved at the next house, and the one after that—a large, two-story wooden structure with creaking floors—is where Miss Bertie lived. She had grown up in this house, but that was several centuries ago. The Morgans lived two houses past Miss Bertie, and at the oak tree in the far corner of their front yard is where my flat world came to an end. If I stepped any farther, I'd fall off the edge.

A lot of the older family homes were along Earlie, before it reached Piedmont and turned into Wellton's main area of commerce. Miss Myers's parents lived a few houses down from my boundary in a home her grandfather had built. I stood on tiptoes to see if I could get a glimpse of her. I didn't see anything but a mailbox, a driveway, and the front steps of the house.

Turning again to face Southview, I discovered a likely prospect for my fold. A collie named Lucy, who belonged to a nearby family, was walking down the sidewalk. "Here, Lucy. Here, girl," I called.

She rushed happily toward me. Patting her head, I asked, "Are you being a good dog? If you do something that we can't see, will we still be proud of you?"

Lucy growled, but, as it turned out, not because of anything I said. When I looked up, I was jolted by an unhappy sight: Ralph was wandering through front yards on the other side of the street. Lucy wasn't happy about this either, and barks were exchanged.

Wanting to ensure my own safe distance, I began to move slowly, taking baby steps toward the Morgans' driveway. I suppose I originally planned to ring their doorbell and drop in for a visit, but Ralph gave a loud bark in my direction. Quickly, I opened the backdoor of Mr. Morgan's Ford Galaxy, jumped in, and slammed it closed. Ralph gave another bark, then eased his way through the Morgans' front yard and started down Earlie. Lucy headed toward her own home.

Breathing easier now, I leaned back. The Morgans would not mind me sitting here for a little while, I thought.

I not only wanted to be certain that Ralph was gone, I also had in my mind that I would conduct a covert operation to see if Pumpkin showed up. If Ralph had gone wandering, this could be the point that Pumpkin chose to follow him. And heading that off here and now would surely go a long way toward keeping Pumpkin on the straight and narrow. I waited to see what would follow.

I had not realized how cool the outside air was until wrapped in the warmth of a vinyl interior. I soon began drifting off to a warm, sleepy land. Sometime later in my dreamlike state, I heard knocking. Why won't someone answer the door? I wondered. Opening my eyes, I turned my head to see Mrs. Morgan's face looking down at me through the backseat window.

"Hannah Hayes, you just about scared me to death," she said as she opened the door. "I was going to the Piggly Wiggly to get some butter for my potatoes, and if I hadn't looked in my backseat, you'd be at the Piggly Wiggly with me. And if I hadn't needed to go to the Piggly Wiggly, you'd probably have slept there all night—and your parents not knowing where you were. You liked to scared me to death."

Mrs. Morgan was a tall, thin woman who seemed, from my backseat vantage point, to stretch all the way to the heavens. With her standing over me in such a state of distress, I misplaced all of my words and couldn't come up with a single explanation for why I was taking a nap in her car.

92

"You're in the car already," she said. "I might as well drive you home."

Mrs. Morgan walked me to our front door, rang the bell, and explained to my mother that she had found me asleep in the backseat of her car and that I almost ended up at the Piggly Wiggly and that if she hadn't needed butter for her potatoes, I might have been there all night. I hadn't been gone long enough for my parents to notice an extended absence, so it was not the absence itself, but the prospect of the night-long separation addressed by Mrs. Morgan that caused so much trouble.

"If she hadn't needed butter for her potatoes," Momma explained to Daddy, "Hannah would have been there all night." Thus, I was on sidewalk restriction for two days. That is to say, I was not allowed to walk or to ride my bike on the sidewalk for two whole days.

As I went glumly to my room to wait for suppertime, I heard the backdoor open.

"Well, there you are, Pumpkin," Daddy said. "We were wondering where you'd gotten off to. Looks like everyone's running late tonight."

Obviously Pumpkin had been up to no good, and this surely had something to do with Ralph. Soon she tapped down the hallway and peered into my room. "You shouldn't run off like that, Pumpkin," I said. "Bad dog. Bad, bad dog."

eleven

S unday night was a church night for many people, but we usually went to those services only on special occasions. I had settled on the couch in the den to watch television when Momma came in and told me to go change clothes.

"Why?" I asked, surprised.

"Robert's getting ordained tonight," Momma explained. "He has asked Franklin to come to the service, so we're all going."

Robert Phillips led a midweek program for boys Franklin's age, and he had been talking to these boys a lot about his call to ministry. Robert was getting his own church this summer, a tiny one in the most rural area of the county, and he also planned to go to seminary in the fall. Before he did all of that, he needed to be ordained by the church thereby obtaining his license to preach.

His ordination service started with a time of testimony to the congregation. Robert stood in the pulpit and talked about how he had been a bad teenager, had fallen in with the wrong crowd, and started drinking alcohol and experimenting with drugs.

"But one day the Lord stopped me cold," he said. "I was at a party and had gotten drunk and was about to drive home, which is so dangerous that I am ashamed to admit it to you. Anyway, I was holding my car keys in my hand, and I was trying to pull the handle on the car door. I was struggling because I'd had so much to drink, and I had a loose grip, which come to think of it, I had a loose grip on almost everything. That's why I was in this kind of state. Anyway, my car keys slipped out of my hands and fell into a grate along the curb of the street where my car was parked. Even sober, I wouldn't have been able to get my keys out. I was pretty mad; I won't say I wasn't mad. And I started kicking my car, which of course didn't help anything. Finally, I got so tired, I sat on the street and leaned against the car and rested. I shut my eyes for I don't know how long, and then I heard this voice say, 'Get up and walk.' I opened my eyes but no one was there.

"'Get up and walk' sounded like a good idea anyway, so I struggled to get up and I started walking home. I was about six miles from home, and walking very slow anyway, so it took a couple of hours to get home, but the whole time I kept hearing this phrase, 'Walk with me.'

"The next morning, I woke up in my bed at home and I wondered a lot of things. I wondered how I had gotten home and I wondered why my feet were so sore. And I wondered who had said, 'Get up and walk.'

"Now, let me tell you, and I hate to admit this, but my mother had been very worried about me. My parents had gotten a divorce a few years earlier and I had taken it pretty hard and she was sure being a good role model—but not a positive male role model and frankly you need both, both male and female role models.

"Anyway, she had prayed for me every day and also left a Holy Bible by my bedside which I had ignored until that morning. So I picked it up and started reading the book of Matthew, and the whole time, I could just sense this, the whole time, I felt the Lord Jesus saying, 'Robert, walk with me.' And that's how I started my Christian walk. I can't say that it's been easy; it hasn't. Since that night I have been trying to do what the Lord Jesus tells me to do, and I have sensed in a very special way that I am being called to Christian ministry.

"I just appreciate this church so much, and I thank you for supporting me and my call to ministry. I love you all and the Lord loves you too. God bless you."

Robert took his seat on the front pew, while Brother John returned to the pulpit. "We will now have the laying on of hands," he announced.

In the laying on of hands, every man in the congregation who had ever been ordained as a deacon or a minister came up front to lay his hands on this man's head. At least twenty men stood at their seats and began to form a file toward the front of the church. One by one they laid their hands on Robert Phillips's head and, it seemed to me, whispered something in his ear. I propped up on my knees to give myself some height.

"Are they whispering something?" I asked Daddy.

"Yes."

"What are they saying?"

Daddy shrugged. "It's a secret."

After the laying on of hands, Brother John was back in the pulpit delivering his message. "We are living in difficult times," he said. "The world is in great need of hope. This is easy to see if you look to all the war and conflict. Look at Vietnam, Southeast Asia. India and Pakistan. Israel and the Arab nations.

"We cry out for world peace, but do we notice the conflicts closer to home? Just last month the Equal Rights Amendment started to make its way through the states. In the coming days we're going to have a lot of discussion about the godly role of women in our families. Some are saying it's time for 'liberation.' I think we must remember that our true liberation—whether we are male or female—is through Christ Jesus.

"As we have roles in our own families, we have roles in the family of God. Some of you may be called to be ministers, like Robert. Some of you may be called to be Sunday school teachers or Bible study leaders. I know that a lot of ladies out there feel a special call to work with children.

97

"Each person has a call," he continued. "You are created for a purpose. And if you are created for a purpose, nothing else will satisfy you. When you're called to serve the Lord, you can run but you can't hide. The only thing in life that will truly satisfy you is to answer the call of God.

"We have seen today an example of answering the call of God. We are all called to God's service, just in different ways. I ask you, as you ask yourselves, if you're called to preach, why aren't you doing it? If you're called to teach, why aren't you doing it? If you're called to give, why aren't you giving?

"I pray that each of you will listen for your call and respond to the Lord's direction in your life. Now let us bless this sacred occasion with prayer."

At the age of seven, I didn't understand what the preacher said about conflicts taking place in other parts of the world, but I did get the message that if you were called to preach, you better do it.

After the prayer and a closing hymn, half the congregation began to file out and half went forward to congratulate Robert at the front of the church. Momma went forward with Franklin while Daddy and I headed toward the parking lot. When we reached our car, Daddy eased in behind the wheel, and I slipped in the back. Leaning forward, I folded my arms on the seat in front. "Daddy," I asked, "can girls get ordained?"

"Well," he said, "I haven't seen that happen, at least not around here. Why do you ask?" He turned the key in the ignition and cranked the car.

"I want to do it," I said.

"I see. Why do you want that?"

"So I can be a preacher."

"Right, a preacher. So you're still thinking about that?"

"Yeah. I want the hand of God on my life," I explained.

"I want that for you too."

"I'm God's witness on earth."

"Yes, you are, and that's an important responsibility."

"So when I grow up, I'm going to be a preacher." I leaned back in my seat, and the conversation rested. Moments later, Momma and Franklin joined us in the car.

"Did you talk to Robert?" I asked Franklin.

"Yeah."

"Did he tell you what they were whispering when they were whispering?"

"What do you mean?" he asked.

"They said something to him when they put their hands on his head. Did he tell you what they said?"

"No, he didn't tell me. You'd have to become a preacher like he is to know something like that."

Nodding, I said, "I'm going to be a preacher."

Franklin shrugged. "They'd have to change all the laws first."

"What laws?"

99

"Right now, they're thinking about making a law where men and women are equal. That means you'll have to go to the boys' bathroom. There won't be girls' bathrooms anymore. They'll all be the same."

Well, Franklin might as well have said the world is ending tomorrow. "I don't want to go to the boys' bathroom!" I protested.

"What's going on back there?" Daddy asked.

"Franklin said I am going to have to start going to the boys' bathroom if they make a law that boys and girls are equal."

"If they do pass a law," Daddy said, "I'm sure we'll be able to work it out like reasonable people."

That was assurance enough for me, and I relaxed. If they did pass a law, we'd be able to work it out like reasonable people.

Momma turned around in her seat. "Hannah, did I hear you say you were going to be a preacher?"

"Yes, ma'am."

"That's sweet, honey. And certainly a lot cleaner than a garbage collector."

twelve

T he school week went by quickly. A Hamilton Sock
Company calendar that Daddy had given me hung
on the wall in my room, and I had begun marking
off the days until school got out for the summer. Before I
had gone to bed, I marked out the Thursday, and I was glad
to wake up to a Friday.

"A bunch of war protesters got arrested," Daddy said as
I walked into the kitchen. "They got into a fight because
they want peace in Indochina."

"It's all madness," Momma said. "Every bit of it."

"Yes, a pervasive madness. Nothing is definitive.
Victory doesn't comfort us, loss is not for a noble cause."

"I just want it over."

"And when it's over," Daddy asked, "what if we find out
that the lawless elements were the good guys?"

"Then they'll win," I interrupted. "The good guys
always win. That's what you said."

Daddy looked up from his paper and watched me pull
a chair to the counter. "Maybe so," he said.

"What's a protester?" I asked as I positioned the dog
food on the can opener.

"It's someone who doesn't like something," Daddy said.

"If I don't like something, am I a protester?"

"Let me clarify. A protester is someone who doesn't like something and carries a sign saying he—or she—doesn't like it." Daddy stood up and took his cup to the counter for more coffee, while Momma said the words that caused my stomach to tighten.

"Let's see who's here this morning."

Nothing I had said to Pumpkin so far had been of any influence, and she continued to allow Ralph to mix with her group of friends. For my part, I couldn't let go of the anxiety caused by Ralph's presence. I didn't want to assume Ralph would be there in the mornings, thus, in some way, willing him to appear. Instead I acted on faith that he would not be there. I kept my routine exactly the same as it had been before Ralph joined the group. As I pulled a chair to the counter and positioned a can on the opener, I maintained a fervent belief that if I acted on faith that Ralph would not be there, he would in fact not be there. All of this was before Momma opened the door. When the door opened, my system of belief was reduced to a yes or no answer. Was Ralph there? Yes he was.

Pumpkin ran in for breakfast, and as I leaned down to pet her, I studied my nemesis through the window. Ralph sat on his hind legs and stared back, in contrast to the other members of the group who milled around pleasantly.

"Daddy," I asked, "do you get arrested if you don't like something?"

102

"There are many levels of not liking something," Daddy said as he sat again at the table. "If you don't like green beans, for instance, and you leave them on your plate uneaten, you do not get arrested. But if you don't like green beans, and you go to the green bean factory and try to destroy it so that there won't be any more green beans, you get arrested."

"What if you just make a sign?"

"Most times signs are okay."

That afternoon I took a sheet of notebook paper and a black marker and made a sign. I was going to write, "Go away Ralph," but I hesitated. For one thing, neither "away" nor "Ralph" had been on my spelling list yet. Two, it seemed unkind. Even though I didn't like Ralph, I didn't want to hurt his feelings or embarrass him among the group. Instead I wrote, "Bad dogs go." Ralph must certainly know he is a bad dog, I reasoned. He should know the sign is for him, and if he has any sense of decency, he will go away.

I took the sign and a Barbie doll to the backdoor. Because I had an early bedtime, I wasn't going to be able to hold the sign all night and wait for the dogs to arrive for their morning meeting. That's why I chose a Barbie doll. She was like a tiny grown-up; she'd be fine by herself at night and outside.

I took the Barbie doll's little hands and pushed them through the paper, creating holes for her to use as grips.

103

Then I stood her upright against the bottom step. Protesters stand, of course. A moment later I thought better of it. Barbie might get tired standing up all night. A sit-down protest might be a better idea. I bent the bottom half of her body and sat her on the step.

The next morning, prompted by a sense of urgency and anticipation, I woke as soon as Pumpkin rolled off my bed. I prayed a desperate prayer that Ralph would not be there, then I carefully followed my routine exactly as it had been before Ralph began to show up. I pulled on a top and culottes, slipped on tennis shoes, and smoothed my hair.

"Someone's up early," Momma said as I walked into the kitchen.

"I had a lot on my mind." I had heard Daddy say that before; it seemed appropriate. I retrieved a can of dog food from the pantry, pulled a chair to the counter, and crawled up to grab the can opener.

"Let's see who's here this morning," Momma said while I concentrated on opening the can. Pumpkin was quickly in the kitchen. When I put the dog food in her dish and could not delay any longer, I looked out the window. Was Ralph there? Yes he was. It was at that moment that I keyed into something significant about the spirit of protest: I didn't care if I got arrested; I wanted Ralph to go away.

The next night, my sign said, "Go awy Raf." Spelling didn't count, it turned out, because Ralph couldn't read.

The protest signs were of no use. Ralph didn't miss a morning club meeting, and I didn't miss a morning prayer for his departure. I couldn't pray for something bad to happen to Ralph, though truth be told, I might not have minded so much. I prayed mostly for him to go away. Sometimes, if I wanted to seem like a good and generous person, I prayed for Ralph to make new friends.

thirteen

On Sunday, we were in our pew in the middle of singing a hymn when Ron Pierce walked in, late as usual, holding the hand of Stella Hamilton. Stella's dress was tight and short; Ron's blond hair was long and wavy. Momma and Daddy raised their eyebrows at each other as the two young people took a seat in the front. Though the music played on in the hands of Mrs. Pierce, I wonder now if within her mirror, from her hidden location in the loft, she could have seen anyone's eyebrows.

Brother John talked about Ron that morning in his sermon. "Our son's eighteenth birthday is not far away," Brother John said. "He's becoming a man. A father takes pride in his son. We also recognize as a family that when our son becomes a man, he will have to assume manly responsibilities. We recognize that when this birthday comes, he'll have to register for the draft.

"I tell you, we don't like to talk about it much in our household. Will the war continue? We do not know. But we hope and pray that these nations may find a peaceful solution to this terrible conflict.

"And what about you?" he asked. "We will all be drafted for some service. Every one of us will face something

106

frightening. Some of America's sons have gone to Canada to avoid fighting what they believe is an immoral war. When your country calls, you can run, but if you start running, you'll always have to run. When your Lord calls, you can run, but if you start running, you'll always have to run." Then he asked us to recommit our lives to the service of the Lord.

Moments later, Franklin and I climbed into the backseat for the drive home. "You're lucky you're a girl," he said.

"How come?" I asked.

"Because you don't have to go to war. They make the boys go, unless they can get out of it."

Even though I didn't understand the full ramifications of Franklin's comment, I did understand the concept that I was lucky to be a girl. I felt so myself. But I was also sensing, little by little, that my luckiness had a few strings attached.

As Daddy cranked the car and pulled out of the parking lot, I watched from my window while other families piled into their cars and filled the roadways of our community. When we were almost to Southview, we passed Miss Myers trimming shrubs in her front yard.

"There's Miss Myers!" I said. I noticed that she wasn't in church clothes on a Sunday, but I didn't have a chance to consider the issue. Franklin was letting his hand rest on my side of the backseat, and he was doing it on purpose.

"Your hand is on my side," I said.

"It's just sitting here."

"It's almost touching me," I said.

Franklin shrugged as he extended his arm over my lap. "I need to stretch."

"Momma! Franklin's arm is on my side."

Daddy responded, "We're only about two feet from home. Can't you two get along long enough for us to get home and eat? I don't like being a referee on an empty stomach."

Lunch was followed by naps for my parents. I was not tired at all, having taken a nap earlier during the church service, but Momma and Daddy were both asleep in the den. Stretched out on the couch, Daddy pretended to watch television, which droned in the background. Momma had fallen asleep sitting up in her chair, pretending to read the Sunday paper spread in her lap. Thankfully for me, Franklin was nowhere in sight, and I was left to my own devices.

Wandering around the backyard trying to think of something to do, I saw Pumpkin and a few of her friends come around the corner. "Hey, Pumpkin," I said. "Hey, y'all. I hope you're up to something good this afternoon."

Maybe they were, maybe they weren't, so I decided that, just to be sure, I'd conduct a revival and help keep them all on the straight and narrow. I crawled on top of the picnic table on our patio to start my sermon.

"Let us remember to be good dogs," I said. "Let us not dig in people's yards or chase cars or kittens. Let us behave at all times."

My pleas did not avail much. The moment a car came down our street, those dogs ran off barking—all of them, even Pumpkin. Franklin came around the corner as I stepped off the table in resignation.

"What are you doing?" he asked.

"I was holding a revival," I said. "But the dogs won't do what they're supposed to."

"I'll be your publicity man," Franklin said. "Now, let's see. We need a way to get them into the backyard. Daddy says the best way to get anybody anywhere is with giveaways."

"What can we give away?" I asked.

"I've got it!" Franklin clapped his hands together, the universal symbol of a brilliant idea. Stepping into the kitchen, he returned moments later with a bag of dry dog food, which he plopped on the patio. Ripping it open, he grabbed two handfuls and started placing the pieces, like pebbles, on a path that led from the front of the house to the picnic table. He grabbed another two handfuls and repeated the process several more times. Soon, the bag of dog food was empty, a number of dogs had been coaxed toward the trail, and I was back on the picnic table preaching.

"And the Bible says, 'Don't take more than you can eat.' Remember there are starving puppies in China. And your eyes are bigger than your stomach."

Still, I couldn't hold my audience. When the food ran out and another car came down the street ripe for the chasing, the dogs were off and running. There was, however, something about our system that seemed effective. Franklin and I wanted to try again, but we were out of dog food.

"We need an offering plate," Franklin said. "We can pass it in the neighborhood and get enough money to buy more dog food."

It seemed like a great idea to me, so I grabbed a marker and some paper and wrote "Ofrin," while Franklin ran inside to get a Frisbee. He taped my note in the front, then placed one of Momma's cloth napkins inside the Frisbee. We set off in the neighborhood, knocking on doors and ringing bells, seeking funding for our ministry.

Next door at the Pattersons', no one came to the door. At the next house, we found Ricky Mann where he often sat when he was home—in a rocker on his porch, enjoying the fresh air and smoking a cigarette.

"Y'all going to be preachers when you grow up?" he asked when we told him what we were doing.

"Yes, sir," I said.

"I better help you out then." A cigarette dangled from his mouth as he reached in his pocket for some change. "Next thing you know, you'll be on some television program giving your testimony, and I want you to say good things about your neighbors. You say we helped you out, okay?"

"We will," I said.

Miss Meadows, a thirtyish woman who was known to like cats better than people, was our next prospect. Four cats swarmed at her feet while she stood at her door listening to us tell of our need to buy dog food for our revival.

"Praise the Lord," she said as she put a dime in our plate. "Those dogs need a revival."

We tried a few more neighbors across the street, receiving several nickels and dimes and a couple of quarters. At Mr. Stevens's house, the last house at the dead end, we stood at the edge of the gravel driveway and thought twice before ringing the bell. The house seemed eerily still and quiet.

"Do you want to?" Franklin asked.

"I guess so," I said.

"If he's down on his luck, he might not have any money," Franklin reminded me.

"You don't think he'll have a dime?" I asked.

"I don't know. He might. We could try and see." Nodding to each other, we went forward to the porch and rang the bell.

"Hey, there, young folks," Mr. Stevens said heartily as he opened the door. "How you doing today?" Except for the stillness and the quietness of the house, he didn't seem all that unlucky. He was clean-shaven and dressed like he had been to church. And he was happy to see us.

"We're fine," Franklin said.

"We're fine," I said.

111

"We're collecting money for a dog revival," Franklin explained. "We're trying to get enough money to buy dog food so that the dogs will want to come hear Hannah preach."

"Yes, sir," I said, "I'm a preacher."

"Well, she's not a real preacher," Franklin confessed.

"You kids are funding a dog revival? I don't think I can pass up an opportunity like that. Might be the best investment I make all day." He reached in his wallet, pulled out a dollar bill and put it in our offering plate. Franklin and I looked at each other with huge eyes. Compared to the other offerings, this was a large amount of money.

"Are you sure, Mr. Stevens?" Franklin asked.

"Maybe it'll bring me luck," he said with a laugh. "I could use all the help I can get."

As Franklin and I left his porch and started the walk home, we counted $1.90 in the collection plate, including the dollar from Mr. Stevens. But news travels fast. As soon as we got home, Daddy knew what we had done and sent us back through the neighborhood to return the money.

"If you want to make money," Daddy told Franklin, "you need to sell a product or a service. At the company we make money, but we sell a product—socks. Don't go to your friends and neighbors and ask them to give you money because you want something. Offer them something that they will think is important enough to pay you money to have it."

112

"Yes, sir," Franklin said. "But what if we give something away?"

"If you give something away, first make sure it is yours to give."

And so we went through the neighborhood again with the nickels, dimes, and quarters. When we got to Mr. Stevens, he took his dollar but seemed disappointed—as if the return of his money meant his luck might not hold after all.

fourteen

I have always been a punctual person. Over the course of my life, if I could not contribute anything else to a situation, at least I could show up at the appointed hour. But I am not perfect, and at least a few times, I have overslept. One of those rare occasions was in the first week of May in 1972. I remember this clearly because I had already marked through the first four days of the month on my calendar. It would be sometime later before I remembered to go back and mark the Friday.

On that morning when my mother told me it was time to get up, I heard her voice say, "Wake up, Hannah. Time to get up," and I felt the disappointment of this news. I didn't want to wake up yet. Then a dream I was having played a trick on me. Something twisted inside my head and told me that her voice had been only a dream. Relieved that my wake-up call had been a false alarm, I rolled over and went back to sleep. In the midst of my comfortable state, however, Momma returned with alarm in her voice: "Hannah, time to get up. You overslept."

Astounded, I jumped out of bed and pulled on a dress laid out on the chair, but I didn't see my shoes and socks. I stepped instead into nearby flip-flops, the fastest shoes I could find. When I walked into the kitchen, my mother's attention was drawn by the slapping of my shoes on the linoleum.

"Hannah, you're not wearing those flip-flops to school," she said. "Go back and put on your saddle oxfords."

"I don't know where they are."

"Find them."

I trudged back to my room, pulled my shoes out of the closet, my socks out of the drawer, and, after reassembling my footwear, returned to the kitchen.

"Much better," Momma said when she saw my shoes. "Get Pumpkin her breakfast, and I'll get yours." I was so late that even Franklin was up and dressed by this time, sitting at the table with Daddy, who was reading his paper.

"Looks like Wallace is sending them a message," he said.

"Who's Wallace sending a message to?" Franklin asked.

"Them," Daddy said.

"Who's them?"

"He doesn't say, specifically. 'Send Them a Message' is his campaign slogan."

"But who's them?" Franklin persisted.

I positioned a can of dog food on the opener while Daddy folded the paper and stood to get coffee from the counter.

115

"When he says 'them,'" Daddy explained as he poured, "he means the people who are not his 'us.' Everybody is somebody's us and somebody's them. The thing is, you'll always see yourself as an us, no matter who sees you as a them. Since everybody is an us, and Wallace is saying let's send a message to them—the ones that aren't us—it's a pretty good slogan." Daddy took a sip of coffee. "In fact, I'd go so far as to say it's a perfect slogan."

"Are you voting for him then?" Momma asked.

"Oh, I don't know," Daddy said. "It might send them a message, and I try to be careful about sending them messages."

The can in my hand completed its rotation on the opener, the top came off with a loud click, and I hopped down from the chair. When I did that, I bumped into Daddy, jostling his coffee but by following the waves with his cup he managed to keep the hot liquid off of him and off of me.

"Let's see who's here this morning," Momma said as she reached for the door. I remember the sound of the door scraping against the door frame as it was pulled open. The sound was supposed to be followed by paw nails tapping on the floor. That's how it always worked; that was our synchronized pattern. But when Momma pulled the door open, no paw nails tapped on the floor, no one rushed in. Instead, Momma stepped outside. "Pumpkin?" she called.

"Is she not there?" Daddy asked.

116

"That's funny," Momma said, walking back into the kitchen. "She loves her breakfast."

Daddy walked out and took a turn calling for Pumpkin. Then he spoke to her friends, "Have any of you fellows seen Pumpkin? Ralph, do you know where Pumpkin is?"

My uneasiness during this moment is another thing I remember; something felt terribly wrong. I had slept late, my shoes had been wrong, and I was now looking through the door at my worst fears fully realized: the presence of Ralph and the absence of Pumpkin. I held the can of dog food tightly in my hand until Daddy removed it and told me to eat my breakfast.

"She'll come around in a little while," Daddy said.

"I'll feed her later," Momma said.

All day at school, I was certain that Pumpkin would be back by the time I got home. She had run off before, although not usually around her breakfast time, but I knew she would return. When Momma picked us up, Pumpkin was the first thing I asked about.

"She hasn't come around yet," Momma said. "She must have gone off on some long adventure."

"Maybe she'll be there when we get home," I said.

"Maybe she will."

When Momma, Franklin, and I pulled into the driveway, I barely let the car coast to a stop before I jumped out.

"Slow down, Hannah," Momma called to my back.

117

Rushing inside, I threw my books on my bed, changed into play clothes—going faster, but otherwise not disturbing my routine, keeping it exactly the same as if I fully believed everything was okay—then I headed to the kitchen. I didn't run, but I walked so fast I practically threw my hips out of joint. When I reached the backdoor and pulled it open, I waited for Pumpkin to rush up and say, "Sorry I missed you this morning." But she wasn't there. No Pumpkin, no dogs at all. I stepped onto the patio and began to call.

"Here, Pumpkin! Here, girl!"

Franklin came around the side of the house. "She isn't here," he said. "I'm going to look."

"Me, too." I yelled into the kitchen, "Momma, I'm going to look for Pumpkin."

"Okay," she called back, "but don't go past the Morgans' house."

Franklin and I set off on separate searches of the neighborhood. I took to the sidewalk, calling for Pumpkin. All through the neighborhood, I checked in ditches and under bushes and looked up and down the road. I returned home through backyards, retraced my steps along the sidewalk, then repeated the process again. I didn't see Pumpkin.

Suppertime posed some distraction, but not much. I couldn't let go of the idea that Pumpkin was missing long enough to concentrate on my peas and carrots. Soon after, when Daddy suggested that I get ready for bed, I did not argue. At least this day was over, and tomorrow Pumpkin would be back.

That night I dreamed I reached the Morgans' house and forgot to stop. I stepped off the sidewalk, and instead of a street, there was a green meadow surrounded by trees. Some distance away, I saw Pumpkin and started calling her and running toward her, but she thought we were playing and ran faster. When Pumpkin reached the end of the meadow, she ducked into the thickness of the trees. That was too far for me to go, and I turned around.

From this angle the meadow seemed much longer and the Morgans' house much farther away. In front of me there was sunlight, but behind me, night was beginning to fall. Without any streetlights on the meadow, I had no warning about this, and with darkness coming, it was time to go home. Though I started running, I couldn't get any closer to the curb of the sidewalk. Exhausted and in a state of panic, I began to cry.

"Hannah!" I was relieved to hear my mother's voice. "Hannah," she said. "Wake up. You're dreaming." I opened my eyes to my mother gently shaking me awake. "Were you having a bad dream?" she asked as she tightened the belt of a robe around a trim waist. Her light brown hair, usually at rest on her shoulders, was captured by curlers.

"I guess it was a bad dream."

"It's all over now."

"Yes, ma'am," I said.

Momma walked back into her room, while I pulled myself out of bed. The dream may have been over, but the anxiety lingered. Pushing it all out of my mind, I pulled on shorts and a T-shirt and walked into the kitchen, to the backdoor, which I opened myself with hope against hope that Pumpkin would be home. There were dogs at the outskirts of the patio—Ralph and three other mutts—but no Pumpkin. Sitting on the back steps, I propped my chin on my fists and my elbows on my knees, and stared at Ralph. He showed no interest in me.

Without Pumpkin in front of me, doubt crept into my soul. She might not come back. Still, I had seen her in my dream. Maybe that was a sign that she was trapped somewhere scary, maybe she was hiding and wanted me to find her, maybe she had run away. Whatever had happened, I needed to bring her back.

As I mulled these possibilities, a thought presented itself: Pumpkin could run but she couldn't hide. With this notion, an echo of Brother John's words, my confidence began to return. An idea of a mission formed in my mind: I would search for Pumpkin, hope for Pumpkin, and keep a watchful eye. But to do this important work, I needed the hand of God on my life. I needed to get ordained—and fast.

Here was my thought: things of God are issues related to eternity. Those closest to eternity must know best about the things of God. Because old people are closest to eternity, they must know the most about God. The oldest person I knew was Miss Bertie. On this Saturday morning, I would look for Pumpkin, but first I would stop at Miss Bertie's house to get ordained.

fifteen

At breakfast I began to form my plan. "Daddy, why would somebody need to get ordained?"

"So that they can have the blessing of the church family," he said as he turned a page of his paper.

"Oh! You just need to get a blessing? I thought you had to get people to put their hands on your head."

"The hands are a symbol of the blessing."

I nodded and took a bite of egg. "How many people have to bless you?"

"You'd want as many as you could get."

"But how many people have to bless you before you can do good work?"

"One, I guess, just to get you started. Then maybe you can get more blessings as you go." He stood up to get coffee from the counter. "Mary, may I pour you some?"

"Yes, thank you," she said. "Hannah, eat up. We've got some muffins, if you want one."

"Yes, ma'am," I said absently; my mind was on blessings. The thing I knew about blessings was what Miss Bertie told me about Jacob and Esau. Jacob tricked Isaac out of a blessing; therefore, it would be okay for me to trick Miss Bertie out of a blessing. Because Jacob tricked Isaac by taking food, a part of the trick would be for me to take food.

"Momma, can I take one of these muffins to Miss Bertie today?"

"Hannah, what a sweet girl you are. Yes, you may. Miss Bertie would like that. And Hannah . . . the word is 'may' not 'can.' You say, 'May I take one of the muffins.'"

"May I take one of the muffins?" I asked.

"Yes, you may."

Traveling through backyards, I arrived at Miss Bertie's back porch where, through the screen door, I could see her sitting at the kitchen table, clipping coupons. The door was a wooden one that had become warped and misshapen over time. When my knuckles knocked on the door, it bounced against the frame in an echo of the knock. Miss Bertie's head bobbed up.

"My goodness gracious, it's Hannah Hayes." She rose slowly and walked toward the door as she spoke through the screen. "What are you doing out so bright and early on a Saturday morning?"

"I brought you a muffin," I said as I held my hand up.

"Bless your heart, child." She opened the door and squeezed my cheeks as hard as she could, which hurt, but I endured it for the cause. Already she had blessed me, or at least blessed my heart; maybe this would qualify as an ordination.

123

"You're a muffin yourself, you're so sweet. Come in this house and see me." As I stepped in, the screen door banged shut behind me, and the loud, sudden noise caused me to almost jump out of my skin.

Miss Bertie's house smelled of ginger and tea and butter and apples. This was the home of a maker of ginger snaps, pound cakes, and pies, and it was never without at least a hint of these ingredients. When Miss Bertie returned to her chair at the table, I took one beside her.

"So what brings you out into the neighborhood this morning?" she asked.

"I've been looking for my dog Pumpkin," I said. "Have you seen her? I think she ran away. Or maybe she got hurt. Or she might be trapped somewhere. I'm trying to find her."

"Bless your heart. I know how that must worry your precious soul."

"Yes, ma'am," I said. This was the second time she had blessed my heart. I supposed this was enough. "I guess I better go look for Pumpkin, Miss Bertie. If she comes around here, will you please let me know?"

"I sure will, Hannah, and thank you so much for this muffin. I know I will enjoy it." As Miss Bertie rose from her chair and took a step, she stumbled from a momentary loss of balance, grabbing my head to steady herself. "My gracious, these old bones don't rise like they used to," she said.

Perfect! I thought. My heart had gotten blessed twice, *and* she put her hands on my head. As far as I knew, this

124

was all I needed to do good work. I said good-bye to Miss Bertie and launched off into the neighborhood as a freshly ordained minister in search of my dog Pumpkin. I walked with confidence and certainty for as far as I was allowed to go, turned around and covered the same territory again, knocking on several doors.

When old man Patterson from next door answered, he looked down at me through a pair of glasses that magnified his eyes. "The better to see you with, my dear" he had said to me once when I asked him why his glasses made his eyes look so big. But this was too important a morning to be distracted by a general concern that my next-door-neighbor was the big, bad wolf in an old man's disguise. Knowing that he was hard of hearing, I cleared my throat and tried to speak up. "Have you seen Pumpkin?" I asked.

"Have I seen something?" he repeated.

"Pumpkin," I said again.

"Something what?"

"Have you seen my dog Pumpkin?"

"Have I been doing something?"

Mrs. Patterson, a short, slightly round lady with a head of white hair, came up behind him. "She's asking if we've seen her dog Pumpkin," she said directly into Mr. Patterson's ear, and turning to me, "No, dear, we haven't. But if we do, we'll send her home."

"Thank you, Mrs. Patterson," I said.

Sylvia Mann was on the street in front of the Pattersons, strolling baby 10K, so I stopped her to ask, "Have you seen my dog Pumpkin?"

"No, Hannah, I sure haven't. But if I do, I'll send her home."

Miss Meadows's car wasn't in her driveway. I passed it by for the porch at Mr. Stevens's house. When I rang the doorbell, there was no answer, which seemed strange to me because his car was in the driveway. I rang again, then again, and finally heard motion inside. When the door slowly opened, Mr. Stevens didn't look so good. His hair was going in all directions, and he was in his pajamas.

"Hey, there, young lady. Sorry it took me so long to get to the door."

"Did I wake you, Mr. Stevens?" I asked, surprised.

"Been working the third shift," he said groggily. "I get home early in the morning and sleep most of the day." He rubbed his eyes and smoothed his hair. "You collecting money for another revival?"

"Oh, no, sir. I can't find my dog Pumpkin. I wondered if you've seen her."

A wave of sadness crossed Mr. Stevens's face. "Oh, baby, I am so sorry," he said. "I'm sorry about your dog. I'll get you another one."

"That's okay, Mr. Stevens. I'll wait for Pumpkin to come back. I know she'll come back. I was just wondering if you've seen her."

"I'll get you another dog, baby."

"That's okay, Mr. Stevens. I'm sorry I woke you up."

His sadness unsettled me; I suppose it reminded me of my own. As I walked from Mr. Stevens's porch, all of those feelings got next to me, and I couldn't shake them. I looked toward Sammy's house and decided against stopping there. He might think I wanted him to come out to play, and this was no time for foolishness.

With a clamminess in my soul, I continued with my mission, walking slowly down Evergreen, turning right onto Southview. I repeated the process three more times, and on this third round when I had gone as far as I was allowed to go, I came to a complete stop in the shade of the large oak tree at the far reaches of my small world. I sat on the curb just to rest and, once still, was overcome by a terrible fear that Pumpkin was gone for good. The loneliness of this moment seemed unspeakable. With chin on folded arms and arms propped on bent knees, I didn't move until a buzzing sound drifted through the neighborhood. Soon the soft glow of streetlights signaled my curfew.

As sad as could be, I stood to walk home. A few steps later, I began to run and, once running, ran all the way to my house, through my backdoor, into the kitchen, into my mother's arms, where I sobbed and sobbed because I did not know where Pumpkin was. And I was afraid she would not come back.

sixteen

On Sunday afternoon to keep me from moping around and staying underfoot, my mother sent me to play at Debbie Sellers's house. Because we were the only two girls near our age on the street, our mothers were constantly conspiring to get us together to play. The playing didn't go as seamlessly as our mothers might have imagined. I wouldn't have said I didn't like Debbie because, as far as I knew, good girls weren't allowed to not like people. But I could see, even then, that Debbie and I saw things differently.

"You'll have fun," Momma explained as she pushed me out the door.

"I don't want to go," I protested. "Franklin doesn't have to go."

"Franklin has boys his own age to play with. Besides, she was nice enough to call and invite you, and it is rude to refuse the hospitality of others."

I trudged toward Debbie's house. Facing the steep driveway, I began the slow climb to the front door. When I rang the bell, Debbie answered.

"My mother made me invite you," she said. "I can have a new book if I play with you this afternoon."

"Okay," I said.

As I stepped into the house, her mother called from the kitchen, "Hello, Hannah, I'm so glad you came to see us."

"Yes, ma'am," I said, following Debbie into the hallway. The walls were lined with photographs of Debbie and her two older brothers. Debbie was what, back then, you called a "late-life" child. Her brothers were much older and already in college. I hardly ever saw them in person.

"Where's your daddy?" I asked.

"He's playing golf."

"Oh," I said, relieved. Her father was large and gruff, and I was scared of him, so that suited me fine.

When we settled in Debbie's room, her first suggestion was that we play house. She wanted to pretend that we were married. I was to be the daddy and go to work, while she rocked a baby doll. I had wanted to be the momma, but she said it was her baby doll, and that it had belonged to her mother, and her mother didn't want her to let other children play with it. With some things you can't argue, so I had to be the daddy. I went to the corner of her room for a few moments, where I pretended that I worked, then I pretended to come back home and say I was hungry. Debbie said she didn't have time to fix my supper because she had been tending to a sick baby all day, and I was going to have to take her out to eat.

"Let's go into the kitchen, really," Debbie said, "and we'll get a snack and pretend that you're taking me out to dinner."

129

The idea of a snack sounded good, so I agreed to the deal. Debbie had lots of snacks. Because of her high metabolism, she said, her mother never cared how much she ate. We went to the kitchen and found some bottled soft drinks in the refrigerator and opened them with a magnet metal opener Debbie lifted off the door. She grabbed a bag of potato chips, and we took our seats at the kitchen table.

"We have to eat in here because I'm not allowed to have snacks in my room."

"Okay," I said.

We sipped and snacked, until Debbie spoke again. "I watched you walk past my house yesterday. All you did is walk. Why were you walking so much?"

"I was looking for Pumpkin."

"Where is she?"

"I don't know."

"What happened to her?"

"I don't know."

"Is she missing?"

"I guess so."

"We read a story at school about a dog that went missing."

"How'd the dog go missing?"

"Oh, it was the saddest thing," Debbie said, leaning close and getting into position for a story. "There was a dog and a master who lived next to a tobacco store. This was great because the master smoked a pipe and had

130

taught his dog to go get him tobacco from the store any time he said the word 'tobacco.' This was okay with the person who ran the store, and this went on for years and years.

"Anyway, one day the master and his dog moved a long, long way away. They packed up their belongings, put them on a truck, and moved to another house two hundred miles away. And they just happened to end up next to another tobacco store. 'That's great!' said the master, so he went next door and told the man who ran the store about his special dog and how his dog always fetched his tobacco for him. So the store owner said that the dog could come get his tobacco and the man could pay later."

"I never heard this story," I interrupted.

"Well, if you knew the story, there'd be no point in my telling it to you," Debbie said, and she continued. "So one day the master is ready to smoke his pipe. He realizes he's out of tobacco, so he says to his dog, 'Tobacco.' Well, the dog looked at his master funny and kind of whimpered. The master didn't know what was wrong because the dog had always been willing to get his tobacco before, so he said again, 'Tobacco, boy. I need tobacco.' Well, the dog whimpered again and kind of tucked his tail between his legs. So the man said again, 'Tobacco, boy. Go get me tobacco.' Boy, was this dog whimpering. Anyway, the dog walked out of the house with his tail tucked between his legs, and he didn't come back."

"What happened?" I asked. "Did he run away?"

"Weeks and weeks went by," Debbie said dramatically, "and nobody saw the dog. The master was so upset. He asked the man at the tobacco store if the dog had been there, and the man said he had never seen him."

"Did he get run over by a car?"

Debbie was milking my interest for all it was worth. "Well," she said with satisfaction, "months went by and nobody saw the dog or heard from the dog, until this one day the master was at home reading a newspaper, and he heard a whimper and a scratch outside his door. He stood up and opened the door, and there was his dog, thin as could be and holding an empty, beat-up bag of tobacco. This poor dog could barely walk inside the house, but he came in slow as could be and fell on the floor with this empty, beat-up bag of tobacco."

I sucked in my breath. "What happened?"

Debbie stretched out her words for emphasis. "Don't you see? He had gone two hundred miles back to the original tobacco store to get his master his tobacco. The master never told him about the store next door. The dog thought he was supposed to go to the old one, and that's why he was so upset. He did go get the tobacco, just like his master told him, but he thought he was supposed to go two hundred miles, instead of just next door. It took him months to do it, but the dog loved his master so much, he did it anyway."

132

I never knew before that a story could cause such a physical reaction. My hand, which had been lifting a potato chip toward my mouth, slowly sank to the table. I felt the presence of a terrible pain in my heart, in my soul, and I was sick to my stomach. Tears stung my eyes, and I was exhausted by an overwhelming sadness that would have never been necessary if only the master had explained to his dog about the store next door.

I almost asked out of habit, "And then what happened?" But I let it go. It was enough to know that a terrible misunderstanding had caused this poor dog to travel a long way away to make his master happy. "Bad dogs go," I had written. And I had told her she was a bad dog. Pumpkin had only done what I asked her to do.

"That's a really sad story," I said.

"Yeah, I know," Debbie said. "I'm going to be a writer when I grow up, so I know."

I nodded, adding, "I'm going to be a preacher."

"A preacher? I don't think girls can be preachers."

"Why not?"

"It's something in the Bible. But you can be a missionary."

"What's the difference?"

"Missionaries go to a foreign country like Africa, and that's where they live."

This comment caused me grave concern. I had no interest in leaving my family and my home and going to a

133

foreign country. "I don't want to live somewhere else," I said as Mrs. Sellers walked into kitchen.

"Hello, girls. Enjoying your snack? Are you moving, Hannah?"

"No, ma'am. Yes, ma'am," I said. "I mean, no, ma'am." Her two questions had come right behind each other, which caused me to mess up my answers, and I didn't know how to make them right again.

"Momma," Debbie said, "Hannah wants to be a preacher when she grows up, but she can't, can she? Girls can't be preachers, right?"

"Well, my word, Hannah," Mrs. Sellers said, moving toward the table. "You certainly have virtuous ambition, but I'm afraid Debbie is right. Women are to remain silent in church. Haven't you heard that?"

"No, ma'am," I said. I had a feeling Mrs. Sellers was teasing me, but I didn't get the joke. As far as I knew, no one was allowed to talk in church. For that matter, Franklin was shushed by my parents as often as I was.

"Oh, yes. That is my husband's all-time favorite Bible verse, but he says you have to have an awful lot of faith to believe it's possible for women to remain silent."

"You do?" I asked.

"Oh, yes," Mrs. Sellers said. "You certainly do."

I was very tired. Remembering what I had said about Pumpkin had made me feel guilty and miserable, and now this line of conversation confused me. There was something about it that made me uneasy. "I think my mom wants me to come home now," I said.

"We are so glad you came to see us today. Aren't we, Debbie?" Mrs. Sellers said. "Tell Hannah you enjoyed her visit."

"I enjoyed it," Debbie said.

"I enjoyed it," I said and moved toward the door.

Back at home, I retreated to my room and fell on my bed. Glancing at the Hamilton Sock Company calendar on my wall, I realized that, though it was now Sunday, I had not yet marked off the Friday before. I remembered again: I had been late, and I had picked the wrong shoes. Earlier, I'd left a sign out. If only I'd done things differently, whatever happened might not have happened.

seventeen

For a time Pumpkin's water dish and breakfast dish, though empty, stayed at the kitchen door. But one day, probably when I was at school, Momma picked those things up and put them away. I don't know when she did it, but I remember when I noticed.

On a Monday a week or so after Pumpkin went missing, when Momma came to the church to retrieve Franklin and me from choir, she had news.

"Wallace got shot today," she said as we drove through the parking lot.

"With a gun?" Franklin asked.

"Yes, he was in Maryland campaigning, and somebody shot him in a parking lot."

I was in the backseat by myself, having deferred to Franklin's size and speed for the front. I pulled myself closer to Momma's ear.

"Is Nixon going to be our governor?" I asked.

"No, honey," she said, "it doesn't work that way. First of all, Wallace was hurt pretty bad, but he is alive. He's still our governor."

Since Wallace and Nixon looked alike to me, I suppose I thought they could stand in for each other when necessary

136

and nobody would be the wiser. But that's not the way it works. Having similar hair color, hairline, and jowls is not reason enough to step into someone else's shoes; shoe size is another matter entirely.

When Daddy got home from work, he and Franklin sat in the den and watched the evening news to find out more about Wallace. Momma was in the kitchen preparing supper, and I was helping her, except that for a moment I was distracted by the refrigerator door. I kept opening and closing it to see if I could figure out if the light turns off when the door is closed, and if so, at what exact point does that happen.

"Close the refrigerator door and keep it closed," Momma said.

"But I was trying to figure out what happens to the light when the door is closed."

"It goes off. That's what happens to it."

In the den Daddy rose from the couch and turned off the television. "It's a shame," he said. "It's a real shame."

"It's a real shame," said Franklin as they both walked into the kitchen.

Daddy grabbed some utensils from a drawer and began to set the table for dinner. "Get the napkins, Hannah," he said. "And take the trash out, Franklin."

Momma leaned over the oven, pulled out a roast, and set it on top of the stove. "It's like the whole world's gone crazy."

"Daddy," I asked, "has the whole world gone crazy?"

"The only world you need to worry about is the one right here," Daddy said. "When you get older, if you want to worry about the rest of the world, that's fine. But for now, you are to worry about being a good girl, getting along with your brother, and doing a good job in school."

"Should I worry about Pumpkin?"

Daddy placed the last knife on the table and looked up. "Hannah, I know you've been looking for Pumpkin. I know it's hard to lose someone you love, but these things happen. It's awful when they do, but it is a part of life. I know it's not easy, but we have to learn to accept that Pumpkin's not coming back."

"But she might come back," I said.

"Honey," Daddy said, "Pumpkin's not coming back, and there isn't anything we can do about it." He had made that statement in a voice mixed with annoyance and concern. He studied the table for a moment, as if he were counting places, or as if he were acting like he was counting places, then he walked toward the cabinet and pulled out four plates.

In my mind the door to Pumpkin's return had been wide open. When Daddy made the statement out loud that Pumpkin was not coming back, he was saying as gently as possible, close the door and keep it closed. I looked toward the floor for Pumpkin's dishes, physical evidence of hope and expectation, and that's when I noticed that they were gone. At that moment, standing at the kitchen table holding a

138

handful of napkins, I closed the door on Pumpkin's return, if for no other reason than Daddy told me to.

When the four of us sat at the table for dinner, Momma asked me to give the blessing. We closed our eyes and bowed our heads, and I gave a blessing I had known since I first knew how to pray: "God is great, God is good, let us thank Him for our food. Amen."

Later that night, I was in my nightgown, under my covers, asking Daddy questions. I had learned early on that, whenever he sat next to me on my bed, the more questions I asked, the longer he stayed.

"Why would somebody shoot Wallace?" I asked.

"I don't know," Daddy said. "I suppose the shooter was out of his mind, maybe looking for attention."

"Was he mad at Wallace?"

"Might have been. Wallace has said some things, and done some things, that made people mad."

"Why would Wallace say things that made people mad?" I rolled on my side, facing Daddy, while he thought of an answer.

"Politicians do that sort of thing," he said. "They say things that make some people angry because those very same things make other people happy."

"What does that mean?"

"Think of it this way. Suppose I were running for an important office, and I made a statement that the girls have

139

to do all of their homework before they can go outside and play, but the boys don't have to do their homework. They can go outside and play whenever they want to."

"That wouldn't be fair!" I protested.

"You wouldn't think so," Daddy said, "but I bet Franklin would think it was a great idea."

"But that's not fair, Daddy."

"Okay, suppose I said it the other way. Suppose I said all the girls can go outside and play whenever they want to, but the boys have to finish their homework first. Would that make you mad?"

"Well, no," I said, cautiously.

"The point I am making is that it depends on your perspective," he said. "It depends on how you see things."

A concern I had stowed for days suddenly found its voice. "Daddy, Mrs. Sellers said girls can't be preachers."

"She did?"

"Yes. And she said it takes a lot of faith to keep women quiet."

"I see. Maybe so but I imagine it takes a lot more faith for women to speak out."

"Then it's okay if I speak out?"

Daddy reached over and patted my head. "If God has whispered something into your soul, I would not hesitate to proclaim it from the mountaintops."

Daddy's words comforted me. I didn't want him to leave yet, so I asked another question.

"Why did Wallace go off like that anyway?"

"He wanted to be president," Daddy said. "When you want something, you can't wait around for it to come to you. You have to go after it. And that's what he wanted."

"Okay," I said, preparing for my last question, the clincher. "Will you tell me a story?

"One quick story," Daddy said, "then it's off to sleep."

And he began to tell about a little girl named Hannah who lived on the moon in a house that was the shape of a sock. She stepped outside one day and, with a basket on her arm, floated around gathering herbs from her garden. That's when she noticed that, many miles away, a large crack was forming on the earth's surface; it was coming apart. So Hannah took out a needle, the largest needle ever made, and she took out a huge ball of thread, the largest ball of thread ever made, and she began to sew the earth back together.

At least that's the part that I remember. Hypnotized by the sound of Daddy's voice, my lids grew heavy, and I was asleep before he finished the tale.

eighteen

The first Friday in June meant the last day of school. Franklin and I carried our good moods home with us when our classes let out. But Momma was testy. While she was in the kitchen preparing for a dinner visit by the Hamiltons, we were in Franklin's room playing "jumping out of a burning building."

Franklin had created stair steps out of his chest of drawers. From top to bottom each drawer was opened a little farther than the rest. I climbed these steps to the top of the chest, or the burning building, and jumped onto Franklin's bed. Franklin, with a plastic fireman's hat atop his head, was directing the rescue.

"You saved me," I exclaimed as I fell onto the bed. But Momma changed the tone when she walked into the room.

"You're both going to need saving if you don't settle down," she said. "You're getting out of hand, and I don't want you messing up this house. Go outside and play."

"But Momma!" we cried simultaneously.

"We're playing rescue," Franklin explained.

"Outside," Momma said. "Go play outside. I don't want you underfoot."

Nothing ruins the spirit of playing outside more than being told that's what you have to do. Franklin grabbed his basketball and shot hoops in the driveway; I sat on the back steps studying the sun. For awhile, I tried to watch this big, bright blob, but the sun never moved. I held up my thumb, to mark its place, though I was soon distracted by a family of bugs crawling on the patio. Grabbing the bug jar I'd left at the backdoor, I placed it sideways on the ground and encouraged the bugs to march inside.

"Welcome to your new home," I said. One bug walked in on her own, but the others needed a push.

Bug relocation gets old after awhile, and I was glad to hear Daddy's car pull into the driveway. Soon I would be released from this long outdoor duty and could get back underfoot. I listened as Daddy pushed the car brake and cut off the engine. His feet scraped up our concrete steps, and he opened the front door. I followed the sound of hard-soled shoes walking through the living room into the kitchen, and I heard murmuring between him and Momma. Three more steps and he pulled the backdoor open and called us in.

"Go change for dinner," he said. "The Hamiltons will be here shortly."

"Okay, Daddy," I said, standing. Before I went inside, I looked up to check the sun's position again. It had moved a whole thumb's length in the sky.

Only the Hamiltons could bring out Sunday clothes on a Friday. Franklin did not have to wear a tie, but he did have to comb his hair and wear long pants and a shirt with buttons. I wore a yellow dress, no sleeves, and white sandals. I loved sandals, although they were bad on my knees—not the sandals, actually, just the fact that whenever I wore them I tended to trip and land on my knees. The space between my feet and the leather of the sandals allowed too much room for error, and the bottom was always getting caught on something. Daddy said I had bad eye-to-toe coordination; wearing sandals obscured my vision.

While we waited for the Hamiltons to arrive, I stood in front of the refrigerator, trying again to find the exact moment of illumination. "And the Lord said, 'Let there be light,'" I exclaimed, pulling the door open. Momma ended my research.

"Close the refrigerator and keep it closed," she said. Closing the door, I walked from the kitchen into the den, where I began to twirl in my dress. I was on my fifth twirl when I suddenly fell prostrate on the floor. There was some connection between my twirls and my landing on the floor, but I couldn't identify it and hadn't yet learned to counter that connection. I stood quickly, so that Daddy might not know I had fallen.

"Are you alright?" Momma called from the kitchen.

"Yes, ma'am," I said.

144

I heard a car door open and slam shut, and another opened and slammed shut in echo. Two people had arrived.

I could usually tell from the house how many people were in a car in the driveway. One door quickly opened and shut meant one person. Two doors quickly opened and shut in succession meant two people. The only confusion was when a door opened and stayed open. That could mean any number of things: An old person was making a slow exit; children were in the car and were unmotivated to get out; or someone had arrived but was evaluating the idea of knocking on the door.

On this occasion, there was no mistaking that two people had arrived. I rushed to the window and saw Mr. and Mrs. Hamilton meet in front of their white Cadillac. Myra Hamilton was a large woman wearing a red linen, short-sleeved shirtdress. One thing about Mrs. Hamilton: her hair never moved. Jet black, teased and heavily sprayed, she wore it like a helmet, as if she placed it on her head each morning and took it off each night. Mr. Hamilton, wearing a suit and tie, as he always had every time I'd seen him, reached for his wife's elbow and guided her up the front steps.

"Everything smells wonderful, Mary," Mrs. Hamilton said as she walked in and hugged my parents.

"You know Franklin and Hannah, of course," Daddy said.

"I sure do. You are both getting so big."

"How you doing there, Franklin?" Mr. Hamilton patted him on his shoulder. "You have a good ball team this year?"

"Yes, sir," Franklin said.

"Now, Mary, do you need any help at all?" Mrs. Hamilton asked.

"No, Myra, I have it all taken care of. May I pour you some iced tea?"

"I would love some."

"If y'all will go relax in the den for a few moments, Hannah and I will take care of everything."

The Hamiltons, Daddy, and Franklin sat in the den, while Momma brought in a tray of iced tea, and I carried in a tray of crackers and cheese.

"Thank you, Mary," Mr. Hamilton said as he took a glass from her tray. "This is so nice of you to have us over." He sipped from his tea, set it on the coffee table, and leaned back in the chair.

"Now, Martin," Mr. Hamilton continued, "you're the publicity man. I was thinking on the ride over, we need some more publicity." He took a cracker from my tray. "Thank you, Hannah."

"What have you got in mind?" Daddy asked, taking a glass from Momma.

"I don't know, something big," Mr. Hamilton said. "Something to get us some attention." Mr. Hamilton reached for his iced tea glass. "Or somebody. Somebody big."

146

"How about Nixon?" Daddy offered. "He's big."

"Yeah, that's funny." Mr. Hamilton chuckled. "You think we can get Nixon to wear our socks?"

"Sure, why not?" Daddy shrugged. "I'm sure Nixon wears socks, and probably our socks. We just need him to say so."

Franklin interrupted. "Can you do that, Daddy?"

"Not really, son," Daddy said, shaking his head. "I'm just kidding. I don't think presidents make endorsements about footwear."

"Yeah, we were just kidding around," Mr. Hamilton said.

"Besides," Daddy added, "Nixon's in the middle of an election right now. He's kind of busy."

"What election?" Mr. Hamilton waved to dismiss the notion. "It's a formality. He'll win in a walk."

"I suppose."

As I held the tray out to Mrs. Hamilton, she took a cracker and said to me, "Thank you, dear. Are you taking in all this important political talk?" She stretched out the word po-lit-i-cal, accenting every syllable.

"Yes, ma'am," I said.

"While we're at it," Daddy continued, "do you want me to see if McGovern will endorse our socks too, assuming he's the one running against Nixon?"

Mr. Hamilton grimaced. "I don't think I'd want some McGovern-voting, long-haired hippie to wear any of our products."

"Well, I wouldn't worry about it. The way I understand it, hippies prefer sandals—and usually without socks."

"Thank goodness for small favors," Mr. Hamilton said.

As I set the tray on our fireplace hearth, so careful not to trip in my sandals, I began to worry that these very sandals might cause the Hamiltons to think I was a hippy. I certainly was not a hippy, however: I was for God, country, and family.

"Too bad about Wallace," Mr. Hamilton continued. "He was making some ground before that tragedy."

Daddy nodded absently. "I guess we'll never know."

Momma set her empty tray on the kitchen counter and returned to the den where she sat for about thirty seconds, listening to a harangue about hippies from Mr. Hamilton.

"With all that hair, you can't tell who's a girl and who's a boy. They don't want to work. They don't want any responsibility. They just want to be 'free' to have 'free love.'"

"Tom," Mrs. Hamilton cautioned. "The children . . ."

"Yes, dear," Mr. Hamilton said, winking at Daddy. "Myra wants me to watch my language in front of such impressionable ears, so I'd best do that. I don't know what I'd do if I didn't have my wife to keep me in line."

Mrs. Hamilton smiled. "It's a full-time job."

"Right. She's got her hands full with me, so she doesn't have time to go off looking for a job like some of those women's libbers."

"Tom . . ."

148

"Sorry, dear," Mr. Hamilton said, laughing. "See what I mean? Full-time job. Oh, Martin, you know that Johnson girl, one of our seamstresses?"

"Amanda?" Daddy asked.

"Yeah, Amanda. Her ne'er-do-well husband showed up this afternoon looking for a handout. Brought their boy with him."

"Arnold," Daddy said.

"Right, and he behaved so badly you can tell already he's going to turn out just like his old man. The acorn doesn't fall far from the tree, I'll tell you."

"They've had a hard time," Daddy said.

"Well, that's because they're lazy."

I had been listening to this adult conversation intently, and suddenly I found my opening to participate. "Arnold's in my class, and he's lazy," I offered.

"Hannah!" my mother exclaimed. Everyone else was silent, looking at me. I was embarrassed, but where had I gone wrong when I was simply agreeing with Mr. Hamilton?

Momma stood and announced dinner. When Daddy rose from his chair, she gave him a look, one of several looks exchanged that evening between the two of them.

We sat in the dining room with the good plates and silver. Momma brought in trays and bowls, and after a quick blessing from Daddy, we began to pass the food around and serve ourselves.

149

"Mary, this is wonderful," Mrs. Hamilton said as she took her first bite. "I don't know how you managed this all by yourself."

"It's a matter of timing and organization," Momma said.

"Yes, isn't everything?" Mrs. Hamilton replied.

I ate quietly, still wondering where'd I gone wrong in my comment about Arnold. The moment I spoke it, I felt right and justified. But once it was out there and I had been reprimanded, I felt ashamed. When things hidden in your heart come out for public viewing, you may not be the good person you thought you were. And the last thing you want is for other people to see that too.

After dinner my parents and the Hamiltons sat in the living room drinking coffee. Franklin retreated to his bedroom, while I moved to the piano and pulled myself onto the bench.

"Do you play the piano, Hannah?" Mrs. Hamilton asked.

"Yes, ma'am," I said.

"What can you play?"

"A few songs my momma taught me. Next year I'm going to take lessons, and then I'll know a lot more and play really good."

"Really 'well,' Hannah," Momma said. "You say 'really well,' not 'really good.'"

150

"Really well, I mean."

"Hannah enjoyed her music class this year," Momma continued. "Evelyn Myers took over when Rita Lloyd went on maternity leave."

"Well, that's nice. Evelyn's a lovely girl."

"Yes, a lovely girl," Mr. Hamilton joined in. "I saw her father this week. He said he had come across some old photographs of his grandfather at our church. He thought I'd like to see them sometime."

"That's nice," Momma said.

"Do the Myerses go to our church?" I asked. I did not remember ever seeing them. Surely I would have noticed.

"No, dear," Mrs. Hamilton said. "They're Jewish. They go to a synagogue in Montgomery."

"They have to go all the way to Montgomery?" I looked at Momma. "Why don't they just go to our church? It's on the street where they live."

"They don't go to our church," Mrs. Hamilton explained, "because they don't believe the same things we do."

"Oh," I said.

"Mr. Myers's grandfather gave the land for the churches," Daddy added. "He owned all that land where their building is now and where the Methodist church and the Baptist church are."

"Why did he do that, if he wasn't even going to go to those churches?" I asked.

151

"He was a generous man," said Daddy. "He wanted to support the community, so he did nice things for others even when they didn't benefit him directly."

Conversation among the adults rested there for a moment, until Mrs. Hamilton broke the pause. "Well, Hannah, are you going to be a pianist when you grow up?"

"I'm going to take lessons and learn to play the best I can," I said. "But I'm really going to be a preacher."

"A girl preacher," Mr. Hamilton interrupted, laughing. "Looks like you've got a little woman's libber here, Martin."

I turned to Momma for guidance. She gave me the "keep quiet" look, and I did. I had a feeling Mr. Hamilton was teasing me, but I wasn't sure if "woman's libber" was a nice phrase or not. Because my comment about Arnold had gone so badly, I dared not risk another.

"You ought to learn to play that piano, and then you'd make a great preacher's wife," Mr. Hamilton said. "Like Mrs. Pierce. A sweet, little girl like you couldn't do any better than that. She doesn't say a word in church, but she plays that organ like an angel."

"Hannah is young still, Tom," Mrs. Hamilton said. "We will have to see what she grows up to be. I think it's time we let Martin and Mary get their children to bed."

Mr. and Mrs. Hamilton rose with their cups and saucers. Momma took Mr. Hamilton's. "Hannah, will you get Mrs. Hamilton's?" she asked.

I began walking toward Mrs. Hamilton, but I forgot to watch what I was doing, and my sandals got the better of me. It started as a simple trip, then I watched almost in slow motion as I fell to my knees, the arms of my parents reached toward me, and Mrs. Hamilton grabbed her cup, which turned on its side and spilled drops of cold coffee on my head.

"My gracious, I am so sorry," Mrs. Hamilton said. She handed the cup and saucer to her husband, while she took her napkin and patted my head dry. "I did not mean to pour my coffee on you, bless your heart."

"You alright, Hannah?" Daddy asked.

"Yes, sir, I'm fine." What a strange night this had been. I had spoken against someone, thinking it was right, but finding out it was wrong. Something in the talk of preaching and piano playing had left me confused. And with that pat, as far as I knew, I had receiving the laying on of hands of the most righteous woman in Wellton, and her blessing to boot.

nineteen

he next morning I was the first one up. Walking through the quietness of the house, I made my way to the kitchen, where I opened the backdoor and stepped outside. Like a person who can't stop staring at a hole, I wanted to make sure Pumpkin wasn't there.

Most of the other dogs no longer gathered at our house—except for Ralph. He sat on hind legs on a slight hill at the far end of our backyard and watched the door. I watched back. Serving as judge and jury for Ralph, I had convicted him of all wrongs. I may have made a sign, but I wouldn't have needed to if it were not for Ralph, so he was the one who had caused Pumpkin to become missing. Why would he be here after all he had done? Is it possible, I asked myself, that Ralph missed Pumpkin too? I sat on the back steps in a staring contest with this enemy dog. I lost. When I heard stirring in the house, I blinked and went inside for breakfast.

After the dishes were cleared, Momma sent Franklin and me outside to play. Franklin ran off to find friends, and I wandered down the sidewalk to the edge of Evergreen, turning right onto Southview, ambling toward the Morgans. I reached the sidewalk's edge and looked toward the Myers house, three houses down from my boundary.

154

I could see a car in the driveway with the trunk open.
A couple of boxes were next to the car waiting to be loaded.
Sitting on the curb, I waited and watched. A few moments
later, Miss Myers walked out of her house with a suitcase
and set it in the trunk. I jumped up and waved.

"Hey, Miss Myers!" She looked up, and I waved again.
"Hey, Miss Myers!"

"Hi, Hannah," she called back. "What a surprise to see
you here. Why don't you come join me for some lemonade?"
She waved me toward her house.

"Yes, ma'am," I said as I broke into a run. It is rude to
refuse the hospitality of others.

"I'm packing to leave," she said, "but I'd love to take a
break with you. Come on in, and I'll pour us a couple of
glasses of lemonade."

Miss Myers lived with her parents in a two-story home
with white columns along a long front porch. We stepped
inside onto dark hardwood floors of a foyer lighted by a gold
chandelier. A baby grand piano in the living room immediately caught my attention. But we went in the other direction.

"This way to the lemonade," Miss Myers said, and I
followed through a dining room decorated with red tapestry,
entering a white and green kitchen with shiny linoleum. I
took a seat in one of the wicker chairs around a round glass
table, while Miss Myers poured two glasses of lemonade.

Miss Myers placed the glasses on the table and took a
seat herself, when a big-eyed cocker spaniel slowly moved

155

across the linoleum. I recognized him as one of Pumpkin's friends, but I had not realized that he belonged to Miss Myers.

"Is that your dog, Miss Myers? I didn't know you had a dog. What's his name?"

"Yes," she said. "That's Samantha."

"Oh, it's a girl dog. I had a girl dog too, but she ran away."

"I'm sorry to hear that."

"Her name was Pumpkin."

"I remember Pumpkin. She would stop by here sometimes in the afternoons."

"Really?"

"Yes, she was a good dog."

"Yes, ma'am, she was."

"You can tell when a dog is from a good family," Miss Myers continued. "I knew Pumpkin was a dog who had been well cared for and who was being raised right. She was a very sweet dog."

"She was a sweet, good dog, but she started running with the wrong crowd."

"And you don't know what happened to her?"

"No, ma'am," I said. "I was waiting on her to come back, but Daddy says sometimes these things happen, and he doesn't think she's coming back."

She nodded, and I sipped. "Are your parents home?" I asked.

"My mother is. She's upstairs dressing. She's not quite as early a riser as you and I are. And my father went to his office for a little while. He'll be home shortly."

A loud groan from Samantha attracted our attention, and we turned to look as she stretched out on the floor. When Samantha's belly pressed against the linoleum, I noticed that she was, bless her heart, fat as a pig. This observation I kept to myself for fear of being thought rude.

"Samantha's a nice dog," I said.

"She sure is good company."

"Ralph is a bad dog. Do you know Ralph?"

"Oh, yes, Ralph. He's a digger. He digs around in my mother's garden. She doesn't like that very much." Miss Myers took a sip of lemonade, and I followed suit.

She wasn't in her dressy clothes today, like she usually wore to school. She was in tennis shoes and a blue cotton jumper, but she still seemed elegant.

"Are you packing to go somewhere?" I asked.

"I'm leaving this afternoon for Birmingham. I have a job. It's not a permanent job, just something for the summer."

"Will you be coming back?"

"Maybe," she smiled.

"I hope so."

"Well, Hannah," Miss Myers said as she stood, "I better finish loading up."

"Okay." I stood too, and we walked from the kitchen toward the front door. When we reached the foyer, I asked, "Will you play the piano, so I can hear it?"

"Actually, I need to be packing right now, Hannah. I'm supposed to leave pretty soon."

"Just one song."

"One song, then. One short song."

We walked into the living room, and Miss Myers took her seat on the bench. She began to play a sweet tune from memory.

"What is it?" I asked, watching her fingers press each key.

"Don't you recognize it?"

"Is it 'Twinkle, Twinkle, Little Star?'"

"Yes, that's one of the first songs I learned as a child. Are you going to take lessons next year?"

"I want to, but I want to be a preacher too. And if you play the piano, they might not let you say anything. Like Mrs. Pierce. She plays like an angel but can't say anything."

"I see," said Miss Myers, standing. "Well, I have every confidence that you'll make the right choice, Hannah."

I hoped so. The question that seemed to keep coming to mind was how to know what made a choice right or wrong. But this question was still vaguely formed; I didn't know how to ask it. So "yes, ma'am," was all I said.

"I need to finish packing now."

As we stepped outside, Miss Myers looked toward the bright morning sun, which promised a day of increasing heat. "Oh, it's going to be a hot one," she said.

"Yes, ma'am." Shielding my eyes, I looked up at Miss Myers. "See you later."

"See you later, Hannah. Have a nice summer." She patted my head, and I started toward the corner. When I turned at Southview, I looked over my shoulder to see if Miss Myers was still watching. She was. I gave a little wave. She smiled and gave a little wave back.

twenty

There have been times in my life when I have had crystal-clear vision, but only when my eyes were closed. In a dream, an idea, a notion, a thought has floated through my mind, creating a form that I looked to for explanation. My eyes opened with a dawning recognition just as the image began to evaporate. Comforted by a presence and haunted by its disappearance, it was in this manner that I saw Pumpkin one last time.

In nightgown and bare feet, on grass moistened by the dew of a summer morning, I plopped down next to my little dog and hugged her close. "Pumpkin, I have missed you," I said. The clouds parted in the summer sky. Streams of sunlight shone down, and I reveled in the warmth.

From a distance, I heard my mother calling and looked to see her standing alone in our driveway. I was trapped by uncertainty, not knowing whether to stay with Pumpkin or to walk toward my mother. Her voice called again; I turned and opened my eyes. In that moment, I was awake and Pumpkin was gone.

"Time to get up, Hannah," Momma said as she looked down at me in my bed.

I rolled over and hung my head off the edge. A solitary stream of sunshine spotlighted Momma's bare feet on the hardwood floor. My eyes left the feet, moved to the blue cotton robe and up to Momma's face. She was a pretty woman, even without makeup—round face, blue eyes, trim figure. She brushed out the rolls in her hair from a night spent in curlers.

"We're going to go see Grandmother Louise today. Remember? Get up, get dressed, and come get some breakfast."

"Okay."

"Is your tooth still in your mouth?"

I felt a front tooth, which days earlier had begun to loosen.

"It's still there," I said.

"Maybe today will be the day."

My only living grandparent, my father's mother, lived in a brick apartment in a section of Birmingham full of old ladies driving big cars to little stores. She had moved there, near my Aunt Frieda and Uncle George, sometime after my grandfather died. The drive to see her took nearly two hours and was spent with Franklin and me trying to get along in the backseat.

"Don't cross this line," he said as he drew an imaginary boundary between us.

"That's not exactly halfway," I protested while drawing another line that seemed more symmetrical with the doors. "You don't cross this one."

"I'm looking out the window anyway. I don't want to be on your side."

After two hours of drawing and crossing boundaries and pestering our parents to find out how much longer, we made the turn into Grandmother's apartment complex.

"Race you to the door," Franklin said as he opened and slammed his door shut and took off along the sidewalk. He pulled open the outer door, let it fall shut, and ran up the steps to Grandmother's apartment.

"No fair," I yelled at his disappearing back. "You got a head start!"

"We're not in any hurry," Momma reminded me as she grabbed my hand and walked with me. Grandmother, standing in the doorway when we reached the top of the steps, was a lady with gray, permed hair who had shrunk to almost the size of Franklin and who wore a housecoat to protect her clothes while she cooked.

"Franklin, you are so big," she said. "And my gracious, look at Hannah."

"Hello, Momma." Daddy gave her a hug.

"Hello, Grandmother Louise," Momma said.

"Come in, come in. I am making us a wonderful lunch, and it will be ready in just a few minutes."

"I've got a loose tooth, Grandmother," I said, catching up with her as she turned toward a small kitchen. She stopped for a moment, cupped my cheeks tightly, and peered into my face as I pressed on the tooth.

"Ohhh, I see that you do."

"Do you want to touch it?" I asked.

"I better not."

The dining room table was in the area between the living room and the kitchen. That's where we gathered while Grandmother placed a plate of roast beef and bowls of green beans and mashed potatoes in front of us.

"When are we going to the zoo?" I asked as we were eating.

"In a little while," Daddy said. He explained to Grandmother, "We told Franklin and Hannah we'd take them to the zoo this afternoon. Do you want to go?"

"Oh, no, I'd rather not walk around that whole place. It's too hot. But y'all go ahead. I know you'll have fun."

After lunch Momma, Daddy, Franklin, and I piled in the car for our afternoon excursion to the Birmingham Zoo, only a short ride from Grandmother's. We visited the lions, bears, and giraffes and rode the train, and the whole time I fiddled absently with my loose tooth.

Next, we bought peanuts for the monkeys and popcorn for ourselves. I grabbed a handful of popcorn from my bag, but when I took my first bite, my front tooth went sideways. I reached to feel its status, and, as I touched it,

163

the tooth came out into my hand. Almost in the same instant, Franklin said, "Let me throw some popcorn," and moved toward my bag. With the instincts of a little sister in danger of having something taken from her, I slung my tooth to hold onto my popcorn. I immediately regretted my choice.

"My tooth!" I screamed.

Momma and Daddy rushed over. "Did you lose it?" Momma asked.

"I dropped it!"

"Where do you think you dropped it?" Daddy asked.

"I don't know. I don't know."

Momma bent down near me and ran her hand over the area, but didn't see it. Soon a number of others were curious about our search, and there were whispers in the crowd, "She lost her front tooth . . . can't find it . . . didn't want to let go of the popcorn." The strangers looked, we all looked, but my tooth was nowhere to be found. Devastated, I broke into tears.

"It's time to go anyway," Daddy said. With a heavy heart, I walked toward the car, and we returned to Grandmother's apartment.

"What in the world has happened to you?" Grandmother asked when she saw my tear-streaked face.

"I lost my tooth and couldn't find it."

"What a shame. You'll get another tooth. One will grow back before you know it."

"But I won't get any money from the Tooth Fairy."

"No, I suppose not," she said.

There was a tradition that, whenever we visited Grandmother, Daddy would run an errand of some sort to get her something she needed, even if she couldn't think of anything she needed. He took her car, too, and filled up the gasoline tank. On this trip, Daddy and Franklin went to get bread and milk while I, exhausted from my misadventures, sat next to Momma on the sofa and laid my head on her lap.

"Those kids sure keep you busy," Grandmother said as she took a seat in a chair beside us.

"They sure do."

With my tongue rubbing the empty place where my tooth had been, my eyelids grew heavy. In a half-asleep state, I listened to the conversation around me.

"You think you'll have any more?"

"I don't know. Martin and I have mentioned it, but two is a handful as it is."

For me, this was an appealing possibility. I wanted a baby in the house that I could hold and rock, especially a little sister. For whatever reason, my parents weren't as committed to the idea as I was.

"I don't know how you feel about this," Momma continued, "but I've thought about getting a job." Had Momma said something about a job? I wondered if I were dreaming, but was too tired to find out for sure.

"Well, I think that's fine—what with Hannah getting older and now in school," Grandmother said. "You young people have so many opportunities. I never thought about being anything other than a wife and mother, and nowadays they say women can be anything they want to be, even president. Why, when I was born, we couldn't even vote!"

"A lot has changed," Momma said. She was quiet for a moment, then began to whisper, but I could still hear what she was saying. "You'll think this is funny. The other day Hannah said she wanted to be a preacher when she grew up."

"You don't say!" Grandmother Louise whispered in return. "I'd like to see how the church would take to that! A girl preacher!"

"Who knows?" Momma laughed. "Maybe it'll be so common when she's grown that no one will say a word."

I was starting to feel sensitive about my calling. For all of my born days, whenever I was in church, I had been told that serving God was the most important thing in the world and that it's what everyone should do. So here I was ready to sign up, and being a preacher was the only way I knew how to say it. But it hadn't escaped my attention that whenever the topic came up, the reaction made it seem like a surprising choice.

"Are y'all talking about me?" I lifted my head.

"We're only saying nice things," Grandmother said.

"Okay," I said, laying my head back down, still too tired to find out for sure.

"Do you miss Wellton?" Momma asked. That was the last thing I remember hearing until the commotion of Daddy and Franklin's return.

"Time to go," Daddy said as he picked me up and carried me to the car, though I was awake by the time we pulled out of the apartment complex. Watching out the window, I waved good-bye to Grandmother, and she waved good-bye to me.

The next morning, when Momma woke me for church, she asked, "Did you hear anything last night?"

"No, ma'am," I said.

"I thought I heard a noise."

"I didn't hear a noise."

Momma turned to walk out of my room. "You better check under your pillow to make sure."

When I lifted my pillow, I was surprised by a shiny new quarter and a short note, carefully printed. "Dear Hannah," the note read, "I found your tooth at the zoo, and I took it. Thank you very much. The Tooth Fairy."

twenty-one

At the end of a long afternoon, I sat on the concrete front porch steps with my chin resting on my knees, listening for Daddy's car. Cars in our neighborhood made different sounds, depending on whether they were automatic or stick shift or depending on the size of the vehicle or the temperament of the driver. Mr. Patterson from next door drove a big car, gunning the engine whenever he turned the corner into our neighborhood. Ricky Mann drove a stick shift Volkswagen; his need to change gears always caused a hesitation at the corner.

I heard these cars and knew which drivers were home, without any need to see them for myself. Instead, I watched a couple of bugs crawl near my bare feet. But when I recognized the familiar, easy pace of my father's Chevrolet Caprice, I looked up. Daddy waved as he turned into the driveway, put the gear in park, and shut off the engine.

"Hi, Hannah," he said, slamming the door and slinging his coat over his shoulder. "Did you have a busy day counting bugs?"

"How'd you know I counted bugs today?"

"I'm a father," he said. "I know things."

We walked inside together and found Momma reading the newspaper on the living room sofa. "Well, hello," she said, "how was work today?"

"It was okay," Daddy said with a shrug.

"Did you get much done?"

"I wrote a memorandum." Daddy laid his coat on the back of a chair and sat down while loosening his tie. I took a place on the sofa next to Momma.

"That doesn't sound like so much work," Momma said as she folded her newspaper.

"It was a memorandum I didn't want to write," Daddy explained. "Doing work you don't want to do takes about ten times as much out of you as doing work you want to do. Therefore, by those standards, today I had ten times my usual workload."

"It's a good thing you're not in charge of payroll," Momma replied. "It would be hard to figure out time-and-a-half based on a standard like that."

"You don't think my numbers add up?" Daddy asked, teasingly.

"I can just hear you telling the workers, 'I don't want to know how long you worked. I want to know how long it *felt* like you worked.'"

"So, if the day seemed to go by fast," Daddy offered, "I'd probably only give them four hours of pay. But if the day seemed to last forever, I'd probably give them time-and-a-half for however long past eight hours that it seemed to last."

169

"Yes," Momma agreed. "That's what you'd do. And if someone said on Wednesday, 'It feels like Friday already,' you'd give them the extra days."

"Now, that does sound like me." Daddy smiled and pointed his finger mockingly at Momma. "You're a very clever girl. But I knew that already. I've known that since the day we met."

"When was that?" I interrupted. "How did you and Momma meet?" I had heard this answer before.

"We met in college," Momma explained.

"She got me through an accounting class. I met her just in time to pass the course."

"Would you have been held back if you didn't meet her?" I asked.

"I'd say so. I would have been held back forever."

"Maybe not forever," Momma said. "Just until the next gullible soul with good math skills came along."

Daddy shook his head. "Now, honey, you know you are the only gullible soul for me, with or without math skills."

"Thank you, dear. You have such a way with words."

"And you have a way with numbers," he said, standing. "You could do something with that, you know. Keep the books someplace."

"I suppose."

"I can ask in the office if there's a need."

"Not at Hamilton Sock Company."

170

Daddy shrugged. "I can't believe what I'm hearing. Obviously, I'm a failure as a PR man if I can't even convince my own wife of my company's good name."

"The company's name is fine. It's just not something that I want to do."

"I guess I'll go change clothes," Daddy sighed.

"And I better start supper." As Daddy walked into the hallway Momma turned to me. "What do you want to do? Do you want to help me with supper, or do you want to run outside and play?"

"I want to run outside and play."

"Then run outside."

"Okay."

Momma stood, holding out her hand to pull me up.

"Momma, what does 'keeping the books' mean?"

"It means getting a job someplace."

"A job!"

"I was just thinking about it, Hannah. Your daddy and I have been talking about it. Nothing has been decided yet."

"Okay."

"Now run outside, and I'll call you when supper's ready."

When I stepped through the front door onto the porch, I found Franklin dragging a refrigerator box into the yard.

"Where'd you get that?" I yelled.

171

"The Manns were going to throw this away," he said. "Can you believe it?"

"But it's a refrigerator box," I said, running toward him. "They're the best."

"I'm going to make a space ship."

"I want to make a house."

"It's my box," Franklin said emphatically. "I'm making a space ship."

"Can I ride in it?" I asked.

"You can ride, but you can't be the pilot. I'm the pilot."

I followed Franklin into the back, where he set up the box on the patio, open-side down. Pulling out a pocketknife, he started cutting a hole in one of the sides.

"This will be the window," he said.

"Let me cut it."

"You're too little. And it's my pocketknife."

"I'm not too little. Let me try."

"It's *my* pocketknife, and I'm the one cutting the window."

As I watched Franklin cut some more, the waiting became unbearable. "Let me have a turn," I persisted. I reached toward the knife, but he pushed my hand away.

From my view of things, I could see that Franklin was cutting down, in a straight line, and would then have to cut across in another straight line. My thinking was that if I could put my hand under his, as he got ready to cut across, my hand would be ready for the knife. At least that's what I was thinking. But as I put my hand in position,

172

something went wrong. I felt a sting, like the worst bug bite ever. When I pulled my hand back, I saw blood.

"You cut me!" I exclaimed.

"You put your hand under my knife," he said.

"I'm hurt!"

"It's your fault!"

I pushed inside the backdoor. "There's blood on my finger," I exclaimed, near tears. Momma grabbed a towel and, pressing it against the cut, guided me down the hallway into the bathroom. She washed it up, put on a bandage, and in the meantime, Daddy took Franklin's knife away.

"If you can't be responsible with it," he said, "you can't carry it in your pocket."

Franklin was still mad when we sat down to supper a short while later.

"It's all your fault," he muttered.

"That's enough," Momma said. "We're going to have a peaceful supper now."

She loaded the plates with potatoes, peas, and chicken, passing them around the table, and for a few moments, we each ate quietly. Momma broke the silence.

"So, anyway, Martin, what was it you didn't want to write about in the memo that took you all day?"

"Oh, that. Tom walked through the factory this morning—I guess to show he was a regular fellow—and he saw that some of our workers have long hair and sideburns.

He came into my office talking about how we had a bunch of hippies at Hamilton Sock Company. Then he announced that we would establish a policy where there would be no long hair and no sideburns and that our employees have thirty days to comply. To be specific, he decided hair couldn't be more than an inch past the collar, and sideburns couldn't grow past the earlobe." Daddy took a bite of chicken. "This is Tom's attempt to prevent the demise of modern society, but I doubt if it produces any more socks."

"Preventing the demise of modern society is a pretty big responsibility for a publicity man," Momma said.

"Yes it is. So, I wrote the memo about ten times, and, finally, this afternoon, it went out under my name."

"This should be interesting."

"Yes, it should," Daddy agreed. "And you're sure you don't want me to see if there's an opening in book-keeping?"

"No, thank you."

Daddy shrugged. "Knock a guy for trying to help his wife find a job."

"Why do you want a job, Momma?" I asked. "Are we poor?"

"No, Hannah," Daddy answered. "It's not the money. We can take care of things on what I earn, and we'll always be able to do that. It's that your mother would like to keep busy, to stay active."

"The extra cash wouldn't hurt," Momma said.

"But it's not the money," Daddy insisted. "It's not about the money. We're doing fine."

"If the women's rights law passes," Franklin interrupted, "all the mommas will have to work. It's going to undermine the home."

Daddy looked cross. "Franklin, do you know what undermine the home means?"

"No, sir."

"So you're simply repeating what someone else told you?"

"Yes, sir."

"And who's been talking to you about the women's rights law?"

"Mrs. Hamilton. She told our Sunday school class that it's important to stand up for what's right, and this is about our homes."

"Well," Daddy said, "Myra Hamilton certainly has a lot on her plate, doesn't she?"

Franklin shrugged, then looked at me and said a frightening thing. "If the law passes, you're going to have to get a job too."

"A job!" I said, dropping my fork on my plate. "I don't want a job!"

"You'll have to get one," Franklin said, matter-of-factly.

"I don't want a job!" I was so tense I could barely breathe.

"A job's not a bad thing, Hannah," Daddy said. "If you find something you really like to do, it gives you a feeling of accomplishment and makes you feel proud. And you get money for doing it."

"You get money?" I asked, breathing a little easier.

"Sure, you do."

Franklin joined in. "I'm going to be an inventor and make lots of money."

"Can he do that, Daddy?" I asked.

"The world is open for Franklin. And a young man has to think about money because he'll support a family some day. But more important than money, a job is a responsibility. When I work, I have responsibilities to the Hamiltons, to our other workers, and to our customers. But I also work because I have a responsibility to you, Franklin, and Momma. I work to be able to provide for you. That means sometimes doing things I don't like. But I wouldn't have it any other way. Because I'd rather do things I don't like than fail to keep my responsibilities to you.

"That was a good speech, wasn't it, honey?" Daddy said to Momma, as he returned his attention to his plate.

"Yes, it certainly was."

"I'm starting to believe it myself." Daddy lifted a fork-ful of potatoes toward his mouth.

His speech was comforting, though limited. Indeed, none of us at the table that night would have had any idea that Momma could one day earn more than Daddy. At the time it wouldn't have seemed possible, just like it once seemed impossible to put a man on the moon. But I did pick up on the theme of responsibility to others.

"Preachers must have the most responsibilities of all," I said.

"You're right about that," Daddy agreed. "Being a preacher is a big job. So is that what you want to do?"

"Yes, sir. I want to be the one in the middle who tells the stories."

"But it's more than that, you know. It's more than telling stories in church. You also have to look out for others, to help them when they need help. Even when you don't feel like it, you have to do it anyway."

"But how would I help anybody?"

"You'd be someone people could turn to if they needed something, like food or clothing or maybe just a kind word. You'd have to be a friend to someone who didn't have a friend."

"Like Arnold Johnson."

"Yes, like that. Are you up for it?"

"Yes, sir," I said. I didn't know exactly what I was agreeing to, but I did understand it as a responsibility that would be mine to keep.

"So it's settled then," Momma said. "We're all getting jobs."

"To jobs," Daddy said, raising his iced tea glass.

"To jobs," we all replied with our own glasses raised.

177

twenty-two

✸

*T*he *Wellton Courier*, a small circulation newspaper delivered five afternoons a week, was being edited by a new man around that time—someone who was even new to Wellton. My memory is that he used the newspaper somehow to pick at the community's sensibilities, and when I say the community, I mean my mother. I interpreted the community's sensibilities in terms of what she liked and didn't like, and she didn't like photographs of car wrecks on the front page.

I was following behind Daddy as he walked into the kitchen with a copy of the newspaper under his arm. "Have you seen this?" He dropped the newspaper on the kitchen table.

"What now?" Momma asked. A photograph of a fender bender on Earlie Street filled the top section; a man was standing next to a car holding a handkerchief to his bleeding forehead. Picking up the newspaper, she said, "Oh, how tasteless. Clay Lewis put another wreck on the front page."

"No, not that," Daddy said. "The article about us."

After the memorandum about the hair policy was issued, a couple of the company's workers grumbled loud enough for a reporter from *The Wellton Courier* to write an article, parts of which Daddy read to Momma.

"The article quotes one of the workers, 'No one in the front office should try to tell us how to live our lives,' said Tim Fuller, a fifteen-year employee. 'It's my hair and I have a right to wear it whatever length I want to.'"

"Funny how Tim got so upset," Momma said. "His hair is as short as yours."

"I know. Listen, here's my quote. 'As president of the Hamilton Sock Company, Tom Hamilton would like to set an example for the community,' said Martin Hayes, director of marketing."

"That's not so bad."

"I bet Tim didn't like it. To him, it's the principle of the thing."

While Momma got supper ready, Franklin and I sat on the den couch with Daddy as he listened to the evening news.

"How do you know if your hair is too long?" Franklin asked.

"You'd have to measure it," Daddy said.

"How are you going to measure it?"

"I'm not measuring hair," Daddy replied, holding up his hands. "Everybody's going to have to measure their own hair. That's one thing you can count on."

I went back to Daddy's earlier comment. "What does 'principle of the thing' mean?"

179

"Standing up for something you believe in," answered Daddy. "But I think you should pick your battles, and I'm not sure this is a battle worth fighting."

"Because his hair is as short as yours is?" I asked.

"Yes," Daddy said. "If he doesn't have long hair, why should he fight a policy that says you should have short hair? Some of the younger people I can understand, but Tim is my age."

"If he's so old, why does he care?" Franklin asked.

Frowning, Daddy looked from the news program to Franklin. "I didn't say he was old. I said he was my age. That is not exactly the same as being old."

Suddenly I thought of something else to ask, a question that had come up recently in another context. "Is he being a friend to someone who doesn't have a friend?"

"What's that?" Daddy asked.

"You know, helping people even if he doesn't feel like it."

Daddy sighed. "You could look at it that way."

Just then Momma called us to supper, and I only had time for one more question. "Daddy, why does Clay Lewis put pictures of car wrecks on the front page?"

Daddy reached to turn off the television. "It catches people's attention, and that's what an editor wants."

"Hannah, put some napkins around the table, please ma'am," Momma said as she put a plate at each place. "And, Franklin, help her with the silverware." Daddy put ice in the glasses, and we soon took our seats at the table.

180

"What'd Tom say about his publicity?" Momma asked.

"He didn't like it very much."

"That's not surprising."

"He doesn't think Clay Lewis has his priorities in order," Daddy continued. "He thinks Clay ought to be supporting the policy instead of giving a few grumblers the opportunity to take potshots. But I doubt if Clay cares anything one way or another about the hair policy. He heard about a complaint, and he ran a story."

"Can't blame him for that," Momma said.

"No, you can't blame an editor for doing his job." Daddy took a bite of pork chop and washed it down with iced tea.

"Stop touching my plate," I said to Franklin. Every time he took a bite he returned his hand to a place right next to my plate. He was doing it on purpose.

"I'm just eating," he said.

Daddy interrupted. "What seems to be the trouble?"

"Franklin's touching my plate, and he's doing it on purpose."

"Relax, Hannah," Momma said. "And, Franklin, keep your hands to yourself."

When we each stood to take our dishes to the counter, Franklin was a step ahead of me, and that could mean only one thing. If he got to the television in the den before I did, he would pick the program we were going to watch. As I hurried to catch up, I heard Daddy telling Momma,

181

"Stella is working at the company this summer. So is Ron Pierce. I see them from my window, spending their breaks together."

"Young lovers," Momma sighed.

"Just like us, honey."

"Except that we're not young anymore."

"Ouch," Daddy said. "This has been a tough crowd tonight."

twenty-three

✦

At the piano, through trial and error, I had picked out the notes for the first two lines of "Twinkle, Twinkle, Little Star." I played them with one finger of one hand over and over until Momma stepped into the living room.

"Hannah, you don't need to be spending your whole Saturday indoors," she said. "Why don't you go play with Debbie or Sammy? Or go see what Franklin is doing on the patio."

"I taught myself 'Twinkle, Twinkle, Little Star.'"

"Yes, I've been hearing that. You have a good ear. But that's enough piano playing for one day, so why don't you run outside now? Get some fresh air."

I slid off the piano bench and moved toward the kitchen.

"But don't come this way. I'm mopping."

"Can I help you mop?" I asked.

"Not today," she said. "I want to do this quickly."

After walking out the front door, I doubled back to the patio to find Franklin. He had laid his refrigerator box out flat and was cutting it into strips with the pocketknife he was allowed again to carry.

"What are you doing?" I asked.

"I'm in the middle of a project," he said.

"Why are you cutting up our space ship?"

"I'm making something."

"What are you making?"

"I'm not telling."

"Let me help."

He looked up from his project and wagged his finger at me. "You're not going to get me in trouble again. I'm busy making something." He returned his attention to the box and began loudly humming a song, but only to annoy me and to let me know that, whatever I said, he couldn't hear because he was humming.

Oh, well. I picked up my bug jar off the window sill and walked around to the side of the house. There were a number of good-sized rocks along this way, and I pulled one back to find a roly-poly resting in the musty dirt underneath. I placed my jar beside the roly-poly and gave it a push toward the opening. The roly-poly curled into a ball and rolled right in, and I screwed the top back on the jar.

As I walked toward the front, I saw that on my side of the street the Pattersons, the Manns, and Miss Meadows all had their sprinklers on. I could picture myself running through one wall of water after another, and I was certain that Sammy would like to run through the sprinklers with me. Setting the jar at the driveway's edge, I followed the

184

sidewalk toward Sammy's, altering my pace to allow the waves from each sprinkler to fall lightly on my shoulders.

With no answer at Sammy's door, I returned along the sidewalk, pausing again for streams of water to pat me on the head. Would Debbie like to walk with me? I wondered. I headed toward her house to find out.

"Would you like to come outside and play?" I asked when she came to the door.

"It's so hot," she replied. "Don't you want to play inside?"

"Okay," I said. If I couldn't play inside my house, I might as well play inside Debbie's house. As we walked toward her bedroom, we passed her parents in the den.

"Hi, Mr. and Mrs. Sellers."

"Hello, Hannah," Mrs. Sellers said. "Nice to see you." Mr. Sellers didn't speak, exactly, but he did nod in my direction.

Debbie and I played with her dolls for a while until she asked if I wanted to get a snack.

"Okay," I said. Thank goodness for her high metabolism.

In the kitchen we sat down at the table with soft drinks and chips.

"I heard a scary, scary story the other day," she said as I sipped from my bottle. "Did you hear about the hatchet man?"

"What hatchet man?"

"I heard about it in school."

185

"What hatchet man?" I repeated.

Debbie took a long sip, then wiped her mouth and began. "Well, what happened was this lady in Birmingham pulled into a gas station and asked for a fill-up. At first the gas station attendant looked at her funny, but he filled up the tank anyway; then when the lady handed him her charge card, he said, 'Ma'am, this card is no good and I'll have to ask you to come inside.'"

"Why'd he do that?"

"That's what I'm telling you. The lady was fit to be tied, she was so mad. 'My card is good and you'll be sorry about this' she was saying when she got out of her car and walked into the office. Anyway, once she got inside, the man explained, 'Lady, I don't know if you know this or not, but there is a bad man crouched in your backseat and he is holding a hatchet.'"

"In her backseat?" I asked, alarmed. "Did she know that?"

"No, she didn't know," said Debbie, shaking her head. "And she almost got murdered just because she didn't look in her backseat before getting in the car."

"Wow." The chip I held in midair dropped on the table.

"You have to eat that," Debbie said. "You can't put it back because you already touched it."

I nodded, putting the chip in my mouth. As we chewed and sipped, I reflected on the story.

186

"Why did the hatchet man want to hurt the woman?" I asked.

"Don't know," Debbie said.

"What happened to him? Did he stay in the car?"

"Don't know."

"Did they arrest him?"

"I don't know," Debbie said, frustrated. "Look, did you like the story or not, because that's the whole story. There isn't anymore. The end, okay?"

"Oh," I said. Regrettably, this was not the last time I would fall for an urban legend. It's the sort of thing that can seep into your consciousness and cause you to spend years checking the backseat of your car before entering. But questions, in time, would help me build a stronger defense. With a true story, there's always more that can be known.

"Would you like to go outside now?" I asked.

"No, but you can go," she suggested.

"Okay. I'll see you later."

I pushed my chair back from the table, placed my empty bottle on the kitchen counter, and headed for the front door. And I admit, as I stepped outside, I nervously looked left and right in case I saw a man with a hatchet.

As I reached my house, I could no longer resist the three sprinklers of my neighbors. Still shooting out walls of water, they stood like hurdles. I broke into a run, leaping through each one and returning by the same process.

187

After three or four round trips, I was soaking wet—and tired too. I lay down on the Pattersons' lawn to rest.

When I'd caught my breath and pulled myself up, my legs and arms and clothes were covered with blades of grass from a freshly mowed lawn. Walking to the backdoor of my house, I stripped off wet clothes and made my way to the bathroom, stepping into the shower. It was, I remember, the first time I took a shower on my own without having to be told that I was dirty. I even knew to wash my hair.

Shortly, in fresh clothes and combed hair, I walked through the house, finding Momma and Daddy talking in the den.

"Tim Fuller is growing sideburns," Daddy was saying. "He told me he's letting his hair grow out."

"Why would he do that?" Momma asked. "He's our age."

"I know how old Tim Fuller is," Daddy said irritably. "He said my father would have done the same thing."

"Oh," Momma replied. "Do you think he would have?"

"I've wondered about that all day. I know he believed in helping people, but I'm not sure if he would have seen protecting hair length as something that was really helping people."

They looked up as I walked in. "Hello, Hannah," Momma said. "Go call Franklin, would you please? It's almost time for supper."

188

"Yes, ma'am," I said. I was struck by their conversation because I had never known Daddy to be confused about something before. He always had ready answers for my questions. But when you're asking a question of yourself that reflects who you are as a person, and who you were taught to be, the answer sometimes takes awhile.

"This hair thing is silly," Momma said to Daddy as I went to find Franklin.

"I do not disagree."

"Do you think it will affect business?"

"No," Daddy said, shaking his head. "Socks sell. It's as simple as that."

Franklin was pulling into the driveway on his bike when I walked out the front door.

"Where have you been?" I asked.

"Town," he said. Pushing his kick stand down with his foot, he stepped off the bike and reached into his pocket. When his hand reappeared, he was holding a couple of dollars and several coins.

"Where'd you get that money?"

"Sold something."

"What'd you sell?"

"Rulers I made."

twenty-four

✦

After church the next day we had Sunday lunch at Snappy's, a local seafood restaurant. I selected the fish sticks. While waiting for my main course to be served, I started in on the crackers and butter, then bread and butter, then the olives off Momma's salad, and washed it all down with a Coca-Cola.

When my fish sticks arrived, they were served with French fries, which I dipped in the cocktail sauce. Afterward, I ate a piece of lemon icebox pie and finished a second Coca-Cola. I couldn't have been happier until I accidentally burped.

"Hannah!" Momma exclaimed, "Excuse you!"

"Excuse me," I apologized. That's when I first noticed that something inside me wasn't working right. I don't know whether it was prompted by the shame of burping in public or of being chastised at the table, but I did notice that something was not quite right.

"Are we all done?" Daddy asked.

"We're done," Momma announced, and we pushed our chairs from the table.

Daddy went to the counter to pay our check, while Momma, Franklin, and I headed for the car. When I sat in the backseat, something still didn't feel right, and I began to feel even worse when Franklin said an awful thing: "Your epidermis is showing."

"It is not!" I responded reflexively. I didn't understand what he said, but I understood by the way he said it that I didn't like it. The energy of my exclamation, however, dislodged something uncomfortable within me. Leaning back, I said, "I don't feel good."

"I guess you don't," Momma replied. "Not with all you ate."

Daddy took his seat behind the wheel, and the car pulled out from the parking lot into the streets of Wellton. To keep myself calm, I began to count the houses we passed, not out loud, just to myself: one, two, three. When we turned onto another street, I lost count and had to start over, which became my new rule. At the start of each street, I started over: one, two, three. I concentrated on the houses as best I could because, deep inside me, I had a nagging fear that if I stopped counting, something terrible would happen.

Soon, we turned into the driveway at home, and I walked into the house with everyone else, wondering what I needed to do to keep myself together, to not feel the way I felt. Daddy moved toward the den, while I followed Momma into the kitchen.

"Oh, Hannah," Franklin said tauntingly. "Your epidermis is showing."

191

"Where?" I asked, alarmed.

When Franklin reached to touch my arm, something about that act loosened every bit of control I had. Suddenly there was a profound rejection of everything I'd eaten for lunch: the fish sticks, the crackers, the olive, the bread. I spewed it all on Momma's clean kitchen floor.

"Ewww . . . !" Franklin exclaimed, covering his mouth and nose. "Gross!"

"To the bathroom," Momma said, grabbing a dishtowel, which she held up to my mouth as she guided me through the hallway. In the bathroom, I vomited once more, this time in the commode. Discarding the dishtowel, Momma took a large bath towel, moistened it on one end, and began to wipe me clean.

"Well, I don't know that all that was caused by too much lunch." She covered my face with her hands. "You may have a bit of a bug. But I don't feel a fever. Do you think anything else is about to come out? Or do you think you got it all?"

"I think I got it all."

Momma pulled my dress over my head. "You stay here and take off your shoes and socks. I'm going to bring you some more clothes."

When Momma returned, I was standing on the bathroom tile in only my underwear. "I'm cold," I said, holding my arms close to my chest.

"I expect you are. Put this on." I pulled on the T-shirt, with Momma guiding my arms through the sleeves, and then I slipped on the shorts. Grabbing another clean towel from the shelves, she said, "Carry this with you to the den. You can rest in there so I can keep an eye on you. And if you throw up, throw up in the towel."

"Yes, ma'am," I said.

"I'll get you some ginger ale to sip on."

"Momma," I weakly proposed as I turned toward the den, "can I help you mop the kitchen floor now?" I was trying to save face, to assure everyone that everything was okay.

"No, dear, I want you to rest right now. You take care of yourself, and you let me take care of the floor."

"Yes, ma'am," I said.

I remembered how confident I was as a non-vomiter the day Arnold Johnson had let loose in the school hallway. Had that been me, I wondered, would everyone else have been as quick to pass judgment?

I suppose vomiting in front of someone is one of the most embarrassing things you can do—not just for yourself, but for the other people too. No one wants to be there when it's time to vomit. But a mother, a mother will stay there until your vomiting is over.

The next day I stayed underfoot at home, still being plied with ginger ale. In the late afternoon, I was at the

193

piano trying to figure out the next set of notes in "Twinkle, Twinkle, Little Star," when Momma walked up behind me, putting her hands on my face.

"You're not warm," she said. "And you haven't thrown up since yesterday. Do you think you're all better?"

"Yes, ma'am."

"Maybe that was the worst of it. Why don't you go outside for a little while and get some fresh air? That might make you feel even better."

"Yes, ma'am," I said.

"Now, don't run around and get hot," Momma cautioned. "Just get some fresh air."

As I went out the front door, I felt as if the warm summer day wrapped its arms around me. My mind was a little fuzzy, and my arms and legs were moving slowly, but I did seem to be better. I spotted my bug jar at the driveway's edge and reached to pick it up. Unscrewing the top, I peered inside for a sight that filled me with anxiety: an immobile roly-poly.

"Move, please, roly-poly," I begged. I did not want this lack of motion to be my fault. I did not want to be the cause of something's demise, yet the evidence was mounting in that direction.

"Roll, roly-poly," I pleaded, as I poked my finger in the jar and gave a push. He rolled, but not with the grace and style as he had previously done. Sighing, I dug my finger in the grass to make an inch-long grave, and I poured my jar's occupant into his final resting place. "I'm sorry, roly-poly," I said, covering him with dirt.

With sadness, I walked toward the patio in back, taking a seat on the steps to rest. The windows to the kitchen were open, and I could hear Momma as she came from the hallway. She was making a nice sound, singing and humming as she moved along. Usually she wouldn't sing or hum in front of anyone, and I wasn't sure if it was wrong to listen to her without her knowing it. I settled my chin on my knees and listened anyway.

The sun heated my legs and arms, and a breeze of warm air waved across my face. Holding on to my jar, I was as still as could be while I listened to Momma. Her singing stopped when we both heard Daddy's car pull into the driveway, a sound soon followed by that of his hard-soled shoes walking through the living room and into the kitchen.

"Where are the kids?" he asked.

"Outside," Momma answered.

"Oh." He dropped something on the counter. "Look what I got at work today."

"What's that?"

"A ruler."

"A ruler?"

"Tim Fuller gave it to me. Seems he ran into Franklin in town on Saturday, and Franklin was selling rulers he'd made."

"Why was Franklin selling rulers?"

"To help people measure their hair."

"Oh," Momma said.

"But his inches are all wrong. He didn't bother with accuracy, so his inches ended up a lot longer than most inches."

"I see."

"And it was the Franklin Hayes measuring system that made them so irresistible in the marketplace. Tim bought four, and he was very glad to give one to me."

"What are you going to say to Franklin?"

"I'm going to say, 'Congratulations on a job well done,'" Daddy said. "And I'm going to tell him if he needs a PR man someday to be sure to keep me in mind."

Something about the warmth of the sun wrapping itself around me made me very relaxed, and before I knew it, my bug jar slipped from my hand and landed with a crash on the patio. It broke in three pieces. When I saw the glass at my feet, I began to cry. I cried because I didn't feel well. Because the roly-poly died. Because my bug jar was broken. Because broken glass was dangerous and shouldn't be next to me. Because I'd listened to my mother sing, and my father talk, when they didn't know it. And because I didn't know what else to do.

twenty-five

I have always liked the sound of rain. I have wondered once or twice how Noah and his wife felt about the sound of rain. Maybe they liked it before they spent forty days on their ark when a flood covered the earth. But I can imagine that after they debarked, they no longer liked the sound of rain.

The house was quiet on this Sunday afternoon, except for the remnants of a soft rain splashing tree limbs outside the bathroom window. I stood on a stool next to the window peering into the mirror, looking to see if my permanent teeth were starting to poke through. How was I to know that these were the last days my face would look this young? My tiny front teeth would be replaced by big ones, which would change my appearance forever.

I hopped off the stool and walked down the hallway into the kitchen. Daddy was on the couch in the den watching an afternoon ball game, while Momma and Franklin had gone off on an errand. With my own business to tend to, I took a seat at the table, where I had left paper and markers, and focused my attention on an unfinished letter. Like Daddy's memorandum, it was a letter I didn't want to write, and it was taking me longer than usual to write it.

197

I had not yet found relief for my guilt, my complicity in Pumpkin's loss, and I had not been able to voice it to Daddy or to anyone else. "Bad dogs go," I had once written in order to protect Pumpkin from Ralph. But I had also told Pumpkin she was a bad dog. Could I somehow make up for what I had said?

"Dear Pumpkin, I miss you," I had written so far. Slowly, letter by letter, I added, "Good dog. Love, Hannah."

That was my message.

My letter was on a single sheet of paper, unfolded and without an envelope, and I took it outside to the mailbox, just as it was. When I stepped off the porch, I could feel the contrast in the weather—the moisture of a subdued rain mixed with the warmth of the summer sun now appearing. I walked toward the street, pulled the handle down, and placed my letter face up in the empty mailbox. When I returned to the house, I fell on the couch next to Daddy.

"Will you play 'Go Fishing' with me?" I asked.

"We can play until Momma and Franklin get home," he said. As he slowly stood, half distracted by the game he was watching, half committed to playing with me, I rushed to the den closet to grab a deck of cards. At the kitchen table Daddy pushed aside my paper and markers, and we took our seats.

"What are we having for supper?" I asked as Daddy dealt the cards.

"I don't know. We'll have to check with your momma when she gets back. You can go first."

I spread out the cards as best I could with my small fingers. "Do you have any eights?"

"Go fishing," Daddy said. I drew a card from the deck. "Do you have any threes?" he asked.

"Go fishing. Do you have any fives?" He handed me a card. "Do you have any fours?"

"Go fishing."

As Daddy was about to ask for a card, we both heard a car pull into the driveway. "Maybe that's them now," he said. One car door opened. I waited for the slam of this door and that of another quickly open and shut. But the door stayed open for awhile, then closed without much emphasis. The sound of heavy shoes scraping the front steps was followed by a knock. Daddy and I abandoned our card game and walked toward the front door; he pulled it open.

"Hello, Ted," Daddy said as he extended a hand. "Good to see you." The hand he shook was Ted Burton's, a man he had known from boyhood.

"How are you, Martin?" Mr. Burton seemed to smile out of habit, but the smile quickly faded. "I'm afraid I've come with bad news."

"Won't you come in?"

Mr. Burton stepped into the house. "Let me tell you straight. Tim Fuller was in a car wreck this morning. He

199

swerved to keep from hitting some trash in the road, lost control, flipped over, and was thrown from the car. He's dead."

"Oh, no," Daddy said softly. "Helen and the kids? Are they okay?"

"They're okay. He was alone. I was going to call, but we've all known each other since we were boys. I thought I should tell you in person."

"I appreciate your coming to tell me," Daddy said. He shook his head. "I'm stunned. I'm speechless. I can't believe it."

"It's a shock. It sure is," Mr. Burton agreed. They both stood there for a moment, not quite knowing what to do. "Well, I'll be going now. I hate to stop in and tell you something awful, but . . ."

"I appreciate it," Daddy said, as Mr. Burton turned to go. Daddy and I walked him to his car. They shook hands again, and we stood in the driveway while Mr. Burton backed out and pulled away. For whatever reason, we all three gave a little wave. I turned to walk toward the house, but Daddy was still for a moment.

"Daddy," I asked, "are you sad?"

"Yes, I am, Hannah. I've known Tim all my life. We grew up together. This is a terrible thing to happen."

When we were back in the kitchen, he said we could keep playing cards. But when we sat at the table, he wasn't the same.

I drew a three. I knew Daddy had threes, but I decided not to ask for any on my next turn. I asked for fives instead, which I knew he didn't have.

"Go fishing," he said.

I took a card carefully—so careful not to disturb the pile, not to disturb this new person. Daddy looked the same, but he was not the same man who had been at the same table a few minutes earlier.

When Momma and Franklin arrived, I heard the normal sound: two car doors opened and shut in quick succession.

"Go wash up for dinner, kids," Momma said as she walked in. Daddy didn't move from the table. "What's wrong?" she asked.

As he began to tell her the news about Tim Fuller, she sat at the table, then reminded us to go wash up. When I walked back into the kitchen a few minutes later, Daddy was still talking to Momma.

"I knew something bad had happened," he said. "I could tell from his voice, from the way he was standing at the door. My whole body tensed up because I thought that he was going to say something had happened to you or Franklin. So when he said it was Tim, at first I was relieved. It was 'only' Tim. Isn't that awful? It wasn't 'only' Tim. It was never 'only' Tim. I feel terrible about what happened, and I feel terrible that my first thought was relief that this bad thing had not happened in my family."

"It was your first reaction, dear. It was natural. It does-n't mean you didn't care about Tim or don't care about his family. It was a terrible thing to happen. And when terrible things happen, you have terrible thoughts. It's only natural."

The next day on the front page of *The Wellton Courier*, there was a photograph of Tim Fuller's yellow Chevy Nova upside down in a ditch. When I saw it, I asked Momma why this had happened. I was looking for a quick answer, a single sentence, not a paragraph, and she gave me one: "He swerved to keep from hitting some trash in the road."

Her explanation moved aside many confusing things. "He swerved to keep from hitting some trash" gave me some blame to place, an "if only." If only he hadn't swerved, this would not have happened.

In 1972, my father was thirty-five years old, and this was not his first experience with death and sadness. When he was twelve, his own father died in a freak accident at Hamilton Sock Company. Howard Hayes had been first-shift supervisor, and in the heat of that summer, twenty-two years earlier, he had climbed a ladder to reopen the vents of a huge fan built into the wall of the factory. The vents had fallen shut when a hinge broke. A repair order was in, but the factory was hot and the workers were complaining. My grandfather climbed to seek a way to prop the vents open. At the top he lost his balance, fell from the ladder, and hit his head on the concrete floor. Seeing this from his

202

glassed-in, air-conditioned office, Andrew Hamilton called an ambulance, suspending operations for the day. He went to the hospital to be with Grandmother Louise and stayed with her until my grandfather died. A few short years later, Andrew would also be dead, killed in a single car accident while driving drunk.

Tim Fuller's death, however, was painful in other ways. For one thing, Tim Fuller was Daddy's age—not paternal, never a guiding force—but as boys, they had been the best of friends.

"If anyone I ever knew was going to die young, it would be Tim Fuller," I heard Daddy tell Momma. "He never took the easy way out of anything."

Something had changed. We'd been talking about Tim Fuller for weeks, and now he was gone, just like that. When everything's the same, you can be quite comfortable talking about others—complaining about them, even saying something like "bad dog"—but when something happens, it sure changes your perspective. It doesn't take half a second to start feeling different.

That night when Daddy sat next to me on my bed, I asked him why Tim Fuller had gotten so upset about the hair thing.

"When you think something is about hair, it's not always about hair," Daddy explained. "Tim believed that the rule was wrong, and he was man enough to say what he felt, so I respect him for that. He had no fear of what might happen as a result. If he lost his job over saying what he believed, that was okay with him."

"Is that the right thing to do?" I asked, rolling onto my side.

"To me, when you know something is wrong, you ought to do something about it. But sometimes the choices aren't as easy as you think they'd be. Good deeds can have serious consequences, and you have to think about what it's going to cost you. Will it cost you your job? Your friends? If it will, you have to be willing to pay that price."

"Oh," I said. He was talking a little bit over my head, but it did register somewhere within that he'd said a good deed could cost me something important. He may have been cautioning me that I better think twice before doing such a thing, but I was hearing that it was my choice. I could choose to pay that price.

"Anyway, that's enough about that. You need to get some sleep."

"Okay, Daddy."

The difficult letter I had written to Pumpkin stayed in the mailbox for three or four days, but the postman kept ignoring it. Perhaps he was a stickler for regulations and would not take my letter without postage, an envelope, or an address. Or maybe he believed someone else should receive my message. That's what came to me when I pulled the letter from the box just as I heard the jingle of a dog collar. Turning to see Ralph coming down the sidewalk, I felt something previously unfamiliar—something like a sense of shame mixed in equal measure with a sense of purpose. Could it be humility?

"Come, boy," I called. "Come, Ralph." As he trotted happily toward me, I reached to pat him on the head. "I'm sorry," I said. "Good dog."

twenty-six

I'd spent most of my Sunday morning standing on the stool in front of the bathroom mirror trying to tie a big, yellow bow behind my back. Frustrated by this difficult task, I set off in search of Momma.

"Tom says the Pierces are leaving," Daddy was saying as I walked into his and Momma's bedroom. "Got a call to another church. An offer he can't refuse."

"Momma?" I interrupted. She was applying her lipstick in front of the dresser mirror while Daddy knotted his tie.

"What is it, Hannah? Are you ready?"

"Will you tie my bow for me?" I asked.

"How about a 'please'?" She put the cap on her tube of lipstick and turned toward me.

"Will you please tie my bow?" I said in compliance.

"Yes, I would be glad to tie your bow."

"So we'll be looking for a preacher," Daddy continued as he reached for the coat laying on the bed. "Hey, how about you, Hannah? You want to be our new preacher?"

"Yes, I do," I said.

"Well, alright," Daddy said. "But I'd like you to at least finish second grade before you go traveling the world on mission."

"Hannah," Momma interrupted, "if you really want to work in a church when you grow up, you'd have a lot of opportunity if you stuck with music, with the piano playing and maybe moved to the organ. Just think. One day you could take Mrs. Pierce's place in the choir loft."

"I don't want to play the organ," I said. The words came out more forcefully than I'd anticipated.

"Well, maybe not now," Momma said. "You can take piano lessons first, and then one day you may find yourself right where Mrs. Pierce once sat."

"I don't want to play the organ," I said. "I want to be a preacher."

"Hannah, sweetie, you can't be a preacher," Momma said. "Girls just don't do that sort of thing. Not around here they don't, so you'd have to go somewhere else, and it could be far away, and I just don't want to think about that. Not this morning, I don't." Momma yanked my bow into a tight knot. "You don't have to decide today. We can talk about it again in a few years. Now get your Bible and get in the car. We don't want to be late."

"Yes, ma'am," I said. I'd heard this idea before. To do God's work, sometimes you have to leave the land and the family that you know. You can't stay where you are. But maybe, if it all goes well or even if it doesn't, one day you can come back home.

207

When we reached the church, we piled out and entered into a tile corridor. Franklin turned right and headed to his class, while Momma and Daddy walked me to Miss Bertie's room before heading to their own class.

"Children," Miss Bertie called my classmates and me to attention. "We only have a short time together now. You're starting school next week, and that means you'll soon be moving to a new Sunday school class too. I will miss you all, but I'm very proud of how much you've grown in the Lord this year."

"Yes, ma'am," a few of us said.

"This morning I want to tell you a story about Jesus," Miss Bertie continued. "We've heard a lot about Jesus this year, and I think you'll like this story too because there's a little boy in it, and he's not much older than you are.

"As we begin the story, Jesus had spent a day preaching and teaching among the people, and a very large crowd had gathered. Because of His miracles and teachings, Jesus was becoming so well known by this time that large crowds would gather around Him. They followed Him wherever He went. At the end of this day, He tried to slip away to rest, but the crowd followed Him.

"Now, He could see that the crowd was as tired and hungry as He was, and He started worrying about them. They didn't have anything to eat. Most people had left their homes that day without packing their lunches. Do any of you, or do your mommas, ever pack your lunch to go to school?"

208

"Yes, ma'am," a few of us said.

"What if you're going on a trip, do you take a picnic basket with you?"

"My momma packed a picnic basket one time," Johnny said, "and Daddy forgot to put it in the car. We had to eat in a restaurant. Daddy said he was going to eat at another table, but he was just joking."

"I see," Miss Bertie said. "Well, let's continue. All of these people had left their homes that day and had forgotten to pack their lunches, except for one little boy—one little boy not much older than you all are. He had packed a lunch with five loaves of bread and two fish. Jesus found out about the boy's lunch, so He asked all the people to sit down, and He took the lunch and gave thanks and started sharing it with the crowd. Each time He would break a loaf of the bread in two, the other half would grow back, and He would break it again. The crowd ended up with plenty to eat that day, so much so that when they gathered the leftovers, they had twelve baskets of food left. And all of this from five loaves and two fish. Isn't that remarkable?"

"Yes, ma'am," we said.

"Now, let's talk about the little boy," Miss Bertie continued. "We don't know his name, but we do know he brought his lunch. Who do you think packed his lunch? Do you think he packed it himself or do you think his momma packed it for him?"

"His momma?" Jerry said.

209

"She might have," Miss Bertie agreed. "Do you think he could bake the loaves of bread himself or did his momma do that for him?"

"His momma," Jerry said.

"What about the two fish? Do you think his daddy caught the fish for him? Do you think his daddy taught him to fish?"

"I've been fishing with my daddy before," Johnny said.

"That's right," Miss Bertie said. "And maybe this boy's daddy took him fishing. His momma probably helped him pack his lunch. And his daddy probably caught the fish for him, or maybe the boy knew how to fish because his daddy had taught him. What I want you to understand is that, before this young boy could share with others, someone else had shared with him. His parents had shared with him. They had taken care of him and provided for him.

"Now, if you have a toy, you might have the toy because someone gave it to you—your parents, grandparents, your aunt or uncle or whoever. Have you ever been asked to share a toy?"

"Yes, ma'am," we said.

"So if you're able to share that toy, it's only because someone else shared first with you, right? Because you wouldn't have it if it hadn't been given to you."

"I got a toy from my grandmother when she came to see me," Cynthia said.

"Yes," Miss Bertie said. "Grandparents like to give to their grandchildren. It is a joyful experience to them. Do any of your parents and teachers tell you to share?"

"Yes, ma'am," we said.

"Is that a hard thing for you do?" she asked.

"Sometimes Franklin wants something of mine, and I don't want him to have it," I answered.

"It's not always easy to share," Miss Bertie agreed. "But sharing is very important. Look at what can happen. When one little boy shared his lunch, Jesus was able to feed five thousand people. Do you see how much can happen when we share?"

"Yes, ma'am," I said. "But Miss Bertie . . ."

"Yes?"

"If someone's had a hard time, do you just give them your food?"

"You can share a lot more than food, Hannah. You can share your friendship and your encouragement. You can also serve as an example to others, so that they'll see by your actions the right thing to do."

twenty-seven

I t was the first day of school, the Friday before Labor Day, and I bounded into the kitchen in hard-soled shoes and a plaid dress with a wide, white collar. Unable to contain my excitement about being a brand new second grader, I bumped into Momma on the way to the breakfast table.

"Careful, Hannah," she said. "I don't want to get anything on my new dress." She'd made the purchase for herself at Earlie's Department Store during back-to-school shopping for Franklin and me the week before.

"Sit down and have some breakfast," Momma said. She placed a bowl of cereal on the table, and I took my place next to Daddy.

"Good morning, Hannah," he said.

"Morning, Daddy."

"You'll want to eat up. You need a lot of energy for the second grade."

"I do?"

"Yes, you do. Second grade uses twice as much energy as first grade."

"Wow," I said, opening my mouth for a spoonful of cereal.

Daddy moved to the counter with his coffee cup. "Mary, are you ready for your interview?" he asked as he poured from the pot.

"I think I am. I'm sure it will go fine."

"I'm sure it will."

"What's an interview?" I asked, with a mouthful of cereal.

"Momma's going to talk with someone about a job this morning."

"You got a job?"

"Nothing has been decided," Momma said. "I'm just talking to someone. And don't talk with your mouth full."

After breakfast I brushed my teeth, then grabbed my pencil and notebook from my room. "Is it time?" I asked Momma as I returned to the kitchen. "Is it time to leave?"

"Go get your brother," she replied.

"Franklin!" I yelled helpfully, but Momma frowned.

"I could have done that myself," she said. When Franklin came into the kitchen, Momma took one look and said, "Tie your shoes."

"Can't he tie them in the car?" I asked.

"No, he needs to tie them now."

I watched impatiently as Franklin deliberately bent down and slowly looped one lace over another.

"Maybe you can get there by noon," Daddy said, stepping into the kitchen. He grabbed his car keys from the counter.

213

"Hurry, Franklin," I prompted.

"I'm hurrying," he replied. But I knew hurrying, and Franklin wasn't hurrying.

"Hannah," Daddy interrupted, "you've got Mrs. Goodman this year, don't you? I had Mrs. Goodman."

"You told me that."

"Oh," Daddy said. "So I did."

"Did you have Mrs. Thomas?" Franklin asked as he pulled a loop tight. "That's who I have."

"No, I didn't have Mrs. Thomas," Daddy said. "She's younger than I am. I couldn't have had her."

"Ready, Franklin?" Momma asked.

"Yes, ma'am," he said, standing. We could finally get going. Walking outside together, Daddy got in his car, while Momma, Franklin, and I got in hers. A short time later, she pulled up to the front of the school and let us out.

"See you at lunchtime," she said.

Franklin and I each waved as we began our trek up the school's sidewalk, but I was the only one of us who repeated, "See you at lunchtime."

The school hallway was filled with the sounds of children excitedly seeking their places at the start of a new year, and I added my voice to the noisy surroundings. Spotting Mrs. Simpson as I made my way up the steps, I yelled, "Hey, Mrs. Simpson!" She smiled and waved back, then held her finger up to her mouth to let me know that I wasn't supposed to yell in the hallway.

Mrs. Goodman, an older woman with a white, beehive hairdo, was standing in the doorway as I got to my room. She greeted us one by one as we entered and told her our names.

"I had your daddy when he was a boy," she said as I introduced myself. "Did you know that?"

"Yes, ma'am," I answered. "He told me."

"Such a sweet boy. I sure did like him."

"Yes, ma'am," I said. It was hard to imagine Daddy as a boy. At Grandmother Louise's, I had seen pictures of him, and I could almost see the daddy I knew in the pictures of the boy, but only in a distorted way.

You'd think that the start of school means crisp, autumn breezes and crunching leaves and all of that, but in Alabama in September, it's still hot. What it really means is that at recess your new clothes itch, and your hair, wet from perspiration, becomes plastered to your beet-red face.

Emily Jeffers and I ran toward the jump ropes. Emily was the kind of girl who, if you didn't want to jump rope with her, didn't let you get a jump rope. It's not that anyone had put her in charge of jump ropes. It's that she had a way of making you think she was in charge. In first grade, because I wanted to be able to get a jump rope when I wanted

215

one, I had done my best to stay on good terms with Emily. In second grade, who's to say whether this would continue?

For much of recess Emily and I had jumped with Cynthia and a couple of other girls. Two of us held the ends of a long rope while the others took their turns, then we switched out. Emily and I were the ones waiting when Arnold Johnson walked in our direction.

"Arnold's coming," Emily said. "Don't look at him."

From her position at a rope end, Cynthia turned to look. "He's really dirty," she said.

I turned myself to see him face to face. At that moment, unexpectedly, something within me changed. It was as though all the things that had happened over the summer—the loss of Pumpkin and reconciliation with Ralph, Tim Fuller's death—had reconfigured my insides, and somehow I was overcome again by that strange feeling of humility.

"Hi, Arnold," I said. He mumbled a hello.

Emily punched me in the shoulder. "Uh oh, you're talking to Arnold," she taunted. "You're going to get his germs!"

I shrugged, not quite sure if my ministry was real. But I was unable to hold off the change that was taking place. "Don't say that," I said, shaking my head. "It's not nice."

The jumping stopped. Emily didn't speak. Arnold didn't speak. Neither did the others. All was silent and still.

"Do you want to jump rope with us, Arnold?" I asked in the quietness. I didn't know if the others would allow this to happen. They might run off with the rope and leave me alone with Arnold. But I couldn't stop myself from asking, even if this good deed made my friends mad at me.

When Arnold shook his head no and began to walk away, this was the first of two responses I had not expected. First, it seemed to me that once I had stepped out there and taken a risk of my own in front of my friends, the logical thing would be for Arnold to accept and appreciate my gesture. I did not know he would decline. Indeed, someone unused to friendly gestures may not recognize friendliness for a long time.

Second, I did not know that someone else could listen to what I had to say. But when something works so powerfully inside you that it creates a change on the outside, people can't help but notice.

"Do you like him?" Emily asked as Arnold retreated from our group. It wasn't an accusation as I might have expected. It was curiosity.

"Arnold's had a hard time, and he needs a friend," I said.

"He does?"

I nodded solemnly.

"But why?" Emily asked.

"See, I get shared things, and Arnold doesn't get shared things, so I have to share things with him.

Somebody has to share with him, because he doesn't have enough of his own stuff, not even enough friends."

"Oh," Emily shrugged.

"It's about God."

"Oh," Emily said again.

"But what about Arnold's germs?" Cynthia asked. "I don't want his germs."

"That's not a nice game," I said. "We can't play it anymore."

"We can't?"

"No, we can't. We have to be nice to him."

"If I have to," Cynthia sighed.

"Nobody can make you do it. But I want to be nice to him now."

"We can be nice to him," Emily said.

Having company in the journey helps. I am reminded that you can't be a fold all by yourself. You always want to get someone else in there with you.

At noon Franklin and I stood in front of the school waiting for Momma. Usually I could see her car right away in the steady stream of cars that pulled up to retrieve schoolchildren. Usually, she was near the front of the line. I stood on my tiptoes to look over the crowd, but couldn't see her silver Caprice. One car pulled up to the front, then another and another and another, and still I didn't see her.

"Where is she?" I asked Franklin.

"She's late," he shrugged.

218

"Late?" She'd never been late before. No one in my family, except Franklin, had ever been late before. "Why's she late?"

"Don't know," Franklin answered.

I stood on tiptoes again to look over the crowd. Straining my neck as high as it would go, I caught a familiar sight of silver. Was that her toward the end of the line? Yes, it was. When it was finally her turn to pull up front, I fell into the backseat.

"Momma, why are you late?" I asked.

"I'm not late," she said. "There are still others behind me."

"I like for you to be in the front of the line."

"Sorry, sweetie, but I'm here now. And I have news. I have a job."

"You do?" I asked.

"Really?" Franklin asked.

"Yes, really. I start in a couple of weeks. This will mean some changes, of course. I may not always be at the front of the line, but I'll get there as soon as I can."

Actually, none of us knew then that Momma was already headed for the front of the line. She would get there as soon as she could, but getting other people behind her did take awhile.

"Hannah," Momma asked as she drove toward home, "how was your first day of second grade? Did you make any new friends?"

219

"I tried," I said.

"You just keep trying then."

"I will," I said. "I'll keep trying."

twenty-eight

❄

Early the next week, Franklin and I spent our after-school hours conducting athletic competitions between the two of us in the front yard. Franklin had won every event, not only because he was older and bigger, but also because he made up the games, and he kept score. After winning the long jump and the ten-yard dash, he was now ahead in the shot put competition. He turned in a circle a couple of times and pushed a tennis ball into the air. The ball flew high, fell quickly, and landed in a sewage drainpipe at the edge of our yard. Franklin rushed over, peering into the long pipe as the ball bounced to a rest well out of reach. Disheartened, he said, "I'm playing in my room now."

This was Franklin's trump card. When he felt like giving me the time of day, we would start a game of some kind, under his direction, and it would be fun. But when he was ready to be done with me, he'd say, "I'm playing in my room." It was of no use for me to get him back by saying, "I'm playing in *my* room," because Franklin had the luxury of being genuinely indifferent. Still, I played the only card I had left.

"I'm going to see Sammy," I said. Franklin's shrug called my bluff, and I had no choice but to go see Sammy. As I

221

reached the sidewalk in front of our house, a car turned onto our street. I glanced behind me to see that Mr. Stevens was coming home. Turning to continue with my walk, I expected the sound of Mr. Stevens's car to reach me soon, certainly by the time I got to Sammy's, but the pace was off. When I turned back to look, he was going so slowly I could have crossed the street five times before he got to where I was. I walked some more, until I reached the point where I needed to cross the street to get to Sammy's. I came to a stop and waited for Mr. Stevens to pass. I gave a little wave when he drove by; he didn't wave back.

As Mr. Stevens turned into his driveway, I ran across the street to Sammy's. Mrs. Morris answered my knock.

"Can Sammy come out and play?" I asked.

"He can come out for a little while," she said. "You're not collecting bugs, are you? I don't want him picking up a lot of bugs. He might get bitten."

"No, ma'am," I said. "I'm not collecting bugs." Just then I heard someone holler behind me.

"Good heavens," Mrs. Morris said. I turned around to see that Mr. Stevens had fallen out of his car.

"I'm fine," he yelled, waving over in our direction as he picked himself up. "Vinyl seats are so slippery," he laughed. We waved back and watched as Mr. Stevens wove his way from his car to the front door.

"That man is such a mess," Mrs. Morris said, shaking her head. "One day you think he's doing all right and the next . . . , well, you just never know what he's going to do."

"Yes, ma'am," I said, agreeably.

"He has a good heart," she continued. "The day he hit your dog, he cried like a baby. But I guess you know that."

I started to say "yes, ma'am" again, out of habit, but "ye . . ." is as far as I got before I realized that I was about to lie to an adult. I did not know that Mr. Stevens had run over Pumpkin. My comment, or lack of comment, didn't matter, however, because it seemed that Mrs. Morris was talking to herself, and I happened to be listening in.

"I had just opened the front blinds to get the morning sun when your little dog ran out in front of his car. Mr. Stevens got out and he was just boo-hooing when he picked her up and put her in the car. He hadn't even been drinking; it was a complete accident."

She looked down at me and shook her head again. "I guess I shouldn't be bringing all these sad memories up when I know you came to play. You want me to get Sammy?"

All of a sudden, without really knowing how to explain why, I no longer wanted to play with Sammy. I had a terrible, overwhelming urge to go home.

"No, ma'am," I said. "I have to go home now."

"Oh," Mrs. Morris answered. "Well, I guess we'll see you a little later."

"Yes, ma'am," I said.

223

I walked toward home, puzzled. Mrs. Morris had given me information that I had not had and did not know if I was supposed to have. I did not know what to do with this new knowledge. Did my parents know but had not told me? Or had Mrs. Morris known and not told them?

It was starting to make sense, however. I remembered when I had asked Mr. Stevens if he had seen Pumpkin. He had said he was sorry, and he seemed truly sad. He had even offered to get me another dog when I was out looking for the one I already had. Was he trying to tell me something I simply could not hear?

As I stepped in the backdoor, Daddy came into the kitchen from the den. "I can't believe that happened," he said, shaking his head. Was this about my dog Pumpkin, I wondered. Did he know?

"It's so awful," Momma agreed. "Hannah, will you help set the table for us?"

"What is awful?" I asked, pulling open the drawer for forks and knives.

"It was at the Olympics," Daddy said. "Something bad happened to the athletes from Israel."

"Oh," I said. This was not about my dog Pumpkin.

Because I was lost in my own reflections, Franklin was paying closer attention to the Olympics than I was. "Why did they do that, Daddy?" he asked as we all sat down for supper.

"The direct reason is that one group of people wanted to get some of their folks out of jail, so they kidnapped another group of people, the athletes, and made them hostages. Then they made demands that their folks be exchanged for the hostages, but a lot of things went wrong, and all the hostages . . . well, they died, they all died."

"They killed them, didn't they, Daddy?" Franklin asked.

"Yeah."

"But why?"

"Franklin, I can't pretend to understand the kind of conflict, religious or otherwise, that causes one group of people to kidnap and kill another group. I'm not going to be able to explain that one to you, but I can tell you this. A lot of things will happen in this world that you are not going to understand. People hurt each other all the time, and sometimes they even tell themselves they're doing it for noble purposes."

The part about things happening that we will not understand piqued my interest, and I joined the conversation. "Daddy, when people do things wrong, when they hurt other people, what do you do?"

"Well, those kidnappers, the ones that survived, will go to jail."

"No, I mean, what if it's someone you know?"

"Oh," Daddy said. He sipped his tea, then wiped his mouth. "Now, if someone has done something wrong that

225

has hurt another person . . . well, let me say this differently. If someone like a friend at school has hurt you by doing something wrong, one thing you might do is go to that friend. You can say that you have been hurt, so your friend will know, but also be willing to offer your forgiveness. Also be willing to say, 'I know you didn't mean it.'"

It did help to think that Mr. Stevens didn't mean to run over Pumpkin. Mrs. Morris had said he was very upset, and I had seen for myself how sad he seemed. Should I go to him and say something about it?

Momma interrupted my thoughts. "Eat up, Hannah. I know you're tired, but you've got to eat up. You need your strength for the new school year."

"Yes, ma'am," I said, forcing a forkful of peas into my mouth.

When we'd finished, I took my plate to the sink. "Can I go brush my teeth now and put on my pajamas?" I asked.

"Yes, you may," Momma said. "You certainly may."

As I walked back to my room, I heard Daddy say, "Hannah's already tired, and it's only her first full week back in school." A little later, he came to my bedroom to tuck me in. Sitting down beside me, he pulled the covers up to my chin.

"Daddy?"

"What is it, Hannah?"

"Nothing," I shrugged.

"Are you worried about the Olympics?" he pressed.

"Munich is a long way away, so there is no need for you to worry, okay?"

"Okay, Daddy."

Truth be told, it wasn't the Olympics I was worried about. That was a long way away, I was a child, and I had no understanding that the death of strangers could affect the lives of people I know or even my own. I was worried instead about what had happened on my street. I was worried about what I was supposed to do or say about Mr. Stevens hurting my dog Pumpkin.

"Daddy, how do you forgive someone if he's hurt someone you love?"

"Oh, Hannah, that's one of the hardest things there is. You see, it'd be a lot easier for me to forgive someone for hurting me than it would be if I had to forgive someone for hurting you. Because I love you, if someone hurt you, it would be very, very hard even to think about forgiving that person."

"Really?" I asked.

"Really. And that goes for everyone else in the house too. You know how Franklin and you pick at each other all the time?"

"Yes, sir."

"Well, even though you pick at each other, you can sure bet that if someone outside this house said or did something to you, Franklin would have a hard time with that. He'd stick up for you, just as you'd stick up for him."

"Really?"

"Yep. Blood is thicker than water, so people fight battles for their family. You can take that awful thing at the Olympics as an example. This is part of a conflict that comes out of really, really big families fighting each other, and it's been going on a long time. Now some more people have been hurt, and you can sure bet their family is going to stick up for the ones they lost. They'll see it as an attack on their family, on people they love, and it's going to be very hard on them."

I knew that something bad had happened, but I had not realized that people were hurting.

"You know the Myerses?" Daddy asked.

"Yes, sir," I said.

"The athletes from Israel were a part of their very big family, and they'll be upset about this. This has hurt them too."

"Really?"

"Really."

I sure didn't know that Miss Myers would be hurt by this too. That made me feel sad.

"Now, that's enough of this for tonight. You need to get some rest. You've got another big day tomorrow."

"Yes, sir," I said, rolling onto my side. "Good night, Daddy."

"Good night, Hannah," he said as he leaned over to kiss my forehead.

228

That had been a lot of information to distill. Scary things were happening in the world and somehow the hurt could reach to my own neighborhood. That's the thing about hurt. It's never contained to one person. It spreads. And this one had traveled all the way from Munich to a house on Earlie Street, to people I knew.

Still, international conflict was too much for my small head to grasp, so I narrowed it down to an understanding of my own street. Mr. Stevens had hurt me when he hurt Pumpkin. That meant it would be much too hard for Daddy to forgive him. This I would have to do on my own.

twenty-nine

Y ou have to be prepared to give up something—maybe a dream, or what you believe about yourself, or even a home—in order to get to the place you need to be. I call it the Conflict of the Concession Stand, an odd phrase on its own. How can you make a concession and take a stand unless you're taking a stand by making a concession? It's the same as losing your life to find it, I think.

On Friday I rose early, pulled on a school dress, and walked into the kitchen. Momma was frying bacon; the sounds of the *Today Show* drifted in from the den; Daddy was at the table drinking coffee and reading the paper. He looked up as I walked in.

"Hannah, you must have something special planned to be up so early this morning," he said.

"I don't have anything special planned."

Daddy looked perplexed. "Are you sure?"

"I think I'm sure." Turning toward Momma for confirmation, I asked, "Do I have anything special planned, Momma?"

"I'm not sure, Hannah," she said. "Do you think Daddy is confusing you with some other little girl?"

Turning back to Daddy, I asked, "Are you confusing me with some other little girl?"

"Well, let me see," he said, placing his fingertips together thoughtfully. "Are you Hannah Hayes?"

"Yes, I am," I said.

"Did you look in the mirror this morning to make sure?"

"No, sir." I had been stumped. I had not looked in the mirror that morning. "But I am Hannah Hayes," I insisted. "I am Hannah Hayes on the inside."

Daddy smiled. "Then you, Hannah Hayes, have something special planned today."

"What do I have planned?"

"You will have to wait and see."

After Emily and I had gotten Cynthia on board, it took a while longer to convince Arnold of our sincerity. We began with the simplest plan: each day, one of us would share something with him—dessert, potato chips, jump rope or whatever. At lunch that day, I had given Arnold the cookies Momma packed for me. And he had accepted and eaten them.

That afternoon in my room I dropped my books on the bed and pulled off my school clothes. I took a quick whiff of a day's activities—the classroom, lunchroom, playground and auditorium. As usual, something of everywhere I'd been attached itself to my clothes and found its way home with me. Would that always be the case? No matter how far my journey might take me, would parts of those faraway places someday return home with me?

As I slipped on a fresh shirt and pair of shorts, I heard a car pull into the driveway. One door opened and stayed open for a good while. A few minutes later, soft shoes padded up the front steps. The doorbell rang.

"Hannah!" Momma called from another room. "Get the door, alright?"

I jumped off the bench and ran to the front door. When I pulled it open, Miss Myers was on the other side holding a small bundle wrapped in a cloth.

"Hey, Miss Myers. Won't you come in?"

When she stepped inside, I wondered if she had brought us a cake or cookies. When her bundle moved on its own, I almost jumped out of my skin.

"I want you to meet someone," she said. She pulled the cover back, and I saw a teeny, tiny dog. "Samantha had puppies this summer."

"Wow!" I exclaimed. "It's the tiniest puppy I've ever seen."

"I can't take care of all the new puppies, Hannah. I wonder if you might take care of this one for me."

"Do you mean it?" I asked.

"Yes, I do mean it," she said.

"I have to ask my mother."

I turned to scream for Momma, but she was already at the door.

"Hello, Evelyn," Momma said.

"Hi, Mary. I was asking Hannah if she might take care of this puppy for me."

"Hannah is quite experienced at taking care of puppies. I'm sure she'd be delighted to do that."

When Miss Myers handed me the puppy, I wrapped my arms around him. His little mouth started gnawing on my fingers. "He's biting me," I said.

"He doesn't mean to," Momma explained. "He's a baby, and he's learning to chew.

While Momma and Miss Myers visited, I focused on the bundle in my arms. I thought of a name—Jack-o'-lantern. That way he would help me honor Pumpkin, but could still grow up to be whoever he wanted to be. I would call him Jack.

Miss Myers soon made excuses about needing to get home, but I think it was not easy for her to leave the puppy behind. I carried Jack as Momma and I walked out to the driveway to see her off. We watched as she backed into the road and straightened her car to drive away, then we all three gave a little wave.

"Momma, can I walk down the street and show Sammy my new puppy?" I asked.

"That would be fine, Hannah. Just be careful with him. Don't jostle him around too much."

"I'll be careful," I said and headed out the front door, down the steps and to the sidewalk. When I reached the point when it was time to cross over to Sammy's, I didn't cross.

I stopped. I hesitated. I debated in my mind and in my heart if I should go to Mr. Stevens's house. I did not know what I would say, what I would do, but I went to the door and rang the bell.

"Well, hello there, young lady," he said when he came to the door. "How are you this afternoon?"

"I'm fine, Mr. Stevens."

"What have you got there?"

"I have a new puppy."

The smile on his face was exchanged for a pale and worried look. "I sure am sorry about your other dog," he said, shaking his head.

"I know you are, Mr. Stevens. I know you didn't mean to hurt Pumpkin. It was an accident."

Mr. Stevens didn't seem to know what to say. He looked like he might cry, but instead he patted my head and nodded ever so slightly.

"Do you want to see Jack?" I asked. Walking into the front yard, Mr. Stevens peered into my bundle to see my sweet new puppy.

"You got yourself a good one there," he said. "And I know you'll take good care of him."

"I sure will. We'd best be going now. You have a good night, Mr. Stevens." I turned toward the sidewalk.

"Hannah," he called suddenly. I turned around. He still looked like he might cry, even though he was smiling now, a real smile. "I sure do thank you for stopping by."

That night Franklin made a doghouse out of a box Daddy brought home from the company. He turned the box on its side, cut some small windows in it so Jack could see, but taped the bottom flap closed to prevent escape. He spread out towels, added a water bowl, then the pièce de résistance, a ticking clock to keep Jack company at night.

While Franklin got the box ready, I held Jack tightly. Because he kept making squeaking, crying noises, I tried to comfort him. "Daddy, he's afraid," I said. "He wants to go home."

"Hannah, he *is* home," Daddy replied. "You just have to let him know."

I took this as an important assignment. I placed Jack gently on the towels and rushed to find some markers and paper. I wrote out four letters which formed a word that created a sign which I taped on the box. The sign said, "Home."

"He'll know he's home now, Daddy."

"Yes, indeed," Daddy said. "He'll know he's home . . . just as soon as we teach him to read."

Acknowledgments

I would like to thank the staff of Paraclete Press for inaugurating the Paraclete Fiction Award; Leif Enger for selecting my manuscript; and Gretchen Jaeger for editing with discipline and grace.

In addition, I would like to extend love and appreciation to Julie, Caroline, Graydon, Meredith, Natalie, and Abby, along with their parents, for inspiration and material; to my late Aunt Minnie for instrumental support; to Wanda and her family for content and counsel; to members past and present of First Baptist Church, Montgomery, for untold kindnesses; and to many others, near and far, for friendship and encouragement.

About Paraclete Press

Who We Are

Paraclete Press is an ecumenical publisher of books on Christian spirituality for people of all denominations and backgrounds.

We publish books that represent the wide spectrum of Christian belief and practice—from Catholic to Evangelical to liturgical to Orthodox.

We market our books primarily through booksellers; we are what is called a "trade" publisher, which means that we like it best when readers buy our books from booksellers, our partners in successfully reaching as wide of an audience as possible.

We are uniquely positioned in the marketplace without connection to a large corporation or conglomerate and with informal relationships to many branches and denominations of faith, rather than a formal relationship to any single one. We focus on publishing a diversity of thoughts and perspectives—the fruit of our diversity as a company.

What We Are Doing

Paraclete Press is publishing books that show the diversity and depth of what it means to be Christian. We publish books that reflect the Christian experience across many cultures, time periods, and houses of worship.

We publish books about spiritual practice, history, ideas, customs, and rituals, and books that nourish the vibrant life of the church.

We have several different series of books within Paraclete Press, including the bestselling Living Library series of modernized classic texts, A Voice from the Monastery—giving voice to men and women monastics on what it means to live a spiritual life today, and Many Mansions—for exploring the riches of the world's religious traditions and discovering how other faiths inform Christian thought and practice.

Learn more about us at our website:
www.paracletepress.com, or call us toll-free at
(800) 451-5006.

If you liked *Life with Strings Attached,* you will also enjoy:

UNVEILING: A Novel
Suzanne Wolfe
190 pages
ISBN: 1-55725-354-4
$19.95 Hardcover

Named one of the
"Top 10 Christian Novels"
of 2004 by Booklist

Still reeling from her recent divorce, Rachel Piers travels to Rome to lead a demanding, art restoration project that could enhance her reputation as a rising star in her profession. As she uncovers layers of grime on what could prove to be a lost Flemish masterpiece, Rachel finds that layers of her own soul are being stripped away.

"With an imaginative vision akin to that of Dante, *Unveiling* probes the myriad layers of meaning in art, the human soul, and ultimately the great world itself. To read this novel is to be reminded that explorations at this depth are inevitably accompanied by uncertainty, suffering, and the piercing joy of revelation."
—Annie Dillard, author of *For the Time Being*—

"This dark and lovely first novel from Wolfe uses themes of faith, brokenness, and redemption to create a memorable work of fiction."
—*Publishers Weekly*—

"A quiet, subtle love story deeply grounded in the restoration of art—and human beings."
—*Booklist* (starred review)—

Available from most booksellers or through
Paraclete Press: www.paracletepress.com; 1-800-451-5006.
Try your local bookstore first.